THE HOLOCAUST AND ANTI-SEMITISM

An Eyewitness Refutal of the Goldhagen Conjecture

Frank Wesley

Heidi VonDalfsen Press

The Holocaust and Anti-Semitism
Revised Edition
Copyright©1998, 2014 by Frank Wesley
All Rights Reserved

Published by
Heidi VonDalfsen Press
(Associated logos and graphics are trademarks of Heidi VonDalfsen Press)
LIBRARY OF CONGRESS CATALOGING-IN-PUBLICATION DATA

Wesley, Frank, 1918.
    The Holocaust and Anti-Semitism: An Eyewitness Refutal of the Goldhagen Conjecture / Frank Wesley.
    p. cm. Includes bibliographical references and index.

    ISBN 978-1-4951-0369-8 (paperback)
    (previously ISBN 1-57309-234-7)

1. Anti-Semitism-Germany-History.
2. Holocaust, Jewish (1939-1945)–Causes.
3. Jews–Germany–History. 4. Germany–Ethnic relations.
5. Goldhagen, Daniel Jonah. Hitler's willing executioners.
6. Wesley, Frank, 1918— .
7. Holocaust, Jewish (1939-1945)—Personal narratives. I. Title.

DS146.G4W47 1998
940.53'18-dc21   97-38775
                                      CIP

Original Copyright ©1998 by Frank Wesley
Revised Edition ©2014 by Frank Wesley

Book Design and Cover Art by
Fran Murphy

All rights reserved. Printed in the United States of America. No part of this book may be reproduced in any manner whatsoever, stored in or introduced into a retrieval system, or transmitted in any form or by any means: electronic, mechanical, photocopying, recording or otherwise, without written permission of the copyright owner and the publisher, except in the case of brief quotations embodied in critical articles and reviews.

Distributed by Heidi VonDalfsen Press
1510 SW 6th Avenue, Portland, OR 97201
For ordering information please visit: www.clean-copy.com

Table of Contents

Commendatory Forewords	vii
Bernard V. Burke	vii
Marshall M. Lee	ix
Introduction	xv

Part 1
Anti-Semitism in Germany   xxi

Chapter 1	Anti-Semitism in Middle Ages	1
Chapter 2	Pre-Nazi Anti-Semitism	7
Chapter 3	The Symbiosis	11
Chapter 4	Hitler's Anti-Semitism	15
Chapter 5	Voting for Hitler	21
Chapter 6	Staged Anti-Semitism	27
Chapter 7	Conditioned Anti-Semitism	33
Chapter 8	Conditioned Brutality	39
Chapter 9	Non-Jewish Victims	43
Chapter 10	Non-German Brutalities	47
Chapter 11	Anti-Semitism Exported	51

Part II
Why No Help   57

Chapter 12	Jews Were Germans	59
Chapter 13	Crushing the Opposition	63
Chapter 14	Power Through Treachery	67
Chapter 15	Entrapping the Jews	73
Chapter 16	Reprisals	81
Chapter 17	Hitler's Irrationality	91

References and Bibliography	99
Appendix	105
Index	147

Commendatory Forewords

Bernard V. Burke
Professor of History
Portland State University

Professor Frank Wesley, a victim of Nazi persecution in Germany, has written a wide-ranging and passionate study of the treatment of German Jews from medieval times through the Hitler era. He has undertaken the task of refuting the notion advanced by D. J. Goldhagen that the German people were willing participants in the extermination of the Jews in Europe. Beginning with medieval times he argues that Germany was no more anti-Semitic than the rest of Europe and then goes on to show that by the nineteenth century Jews in Germany were accorded equal rights and protection in the law. That protection was so deeply ingrained among German Jews that Wesley and his fellow Jews believed that their rights would be guaranteed as long as they followed the law and they held on to those beliefs right up to the time they arrived at the concentration camp at Buchenwald.

Wesley contends that the Jews had "an intimate and reciprocally satisfying relationship" with Germans from the Second Empire through the Weimar era. He points to the numerous Jews who played prominent roles in German politics and culture and makes clear that Hitler's anti-Semitism was derived from French and British writers.

Although he would suffer directly from Nazi animus toward Jews, Wesley recalls that he and fellow Jews did not react with alarm at hearing Hitler's viciously anti-Semitic speeches. The Nazi was considered to be another "Gutter", Jew baiter, among those who had never been successful in Germany. It was rather like listening to the "development of a psychosis, somewhat like listening to an anti-Semitic rap artist without taking the drumming rhythm personally."

When Hitler dominated Germany there were regularly staged demonstrations and much anti-Semitic propaganda but Wesley maintains that the din of hatred did not significantly change the relationship between German Jews and Gentiles nor did it alter his personal friendships.

Without stinting in his description of the horrors of the concentration camp, Wesley cogently argues against Goldhagen's assertion that the sadistic conduct of camp guards stemmed from innate German anti-Semitism. Instead, he shows that such brutality was the result of "centralized training of the guards." He makes his argument more compelling by explaining that non-Jews were also victims as well, perpetrators of the atrocities of the camps and, in a fascinating twist, Wesley shows that Hitler was more successful in exporting anti-Semitism abroad than he was in spreading the hatred at home.

In sometimes chilling prose, Wesley tells the story of the Nazi persecution of the Jews, but from personal experience and deeply held pride in being German, he is able to exonerate the German people as a whole from the atrocities perpetuated in their name. From the perspective of a prominent psychologist, his analysis is telling and, at the same time, his account is personal and compelling, a tour de force which helps us to understand the conflicted memories and experiences of German Jews in the Nazi era.

Marshall M. Lee
Pacific University
Forest Grove, Oregon

The Goldhagen controversy sails on. The appearance of Daniel J. Goldhagen's *Hitler's Willing Executioners* in 1996 opened old wounds, slashed new ones and sparked a scholarly and popular debate that has yet to subside.[1] In all, Goldhagen boldly claimed to have broken new ground, brushing aside almost a half a century of scholarship and leaving in his wake the world's greatest Holocaust scholars gasping, not at his conclusions, but at his insouciance. Dismissing the work of such venerable scholars as Raul Hilberg, Yehuda Bauer, and Karl Schleunes, as well as that of the more recent generations' leading lights, Christopher Browning, Richard Breitman and Omar Bartov, Goldhagen claims to be the first Holocaust scholar to do significant work in German Federal court records of the trails of Holocaust perpetrators; he claims to have developed what he calls a "cognitive mode" of German behavior.[2]

Goldhagen's book has received two distinctly different responses. From the wider public, Goldhagen has been generally well received, since he offers a deceptively simple explanation for bewilderingly complex events. From scholars in his field, however, his reception has been far less cordial. And most recently, reviews by Ruth Bettina Birn and Norman G. Finkelstein have renewed the widespread professional criticism of Goldhagen's methods, his sources and his conclusions.[3] Goldhagen has chosen not to respond in writing to his most recent critics; he has chosen, rather, to pursue legal action against them in London, a course of

---

[1] Daniel Jonah Goldhagen, *Hitler's Willing Executioners: Ordinary Germans and the Holocaust* (New York, 1996).
[2] Raul Hilberg, *The Destruction of the European Jews* (New York, 1961); *A History of the Holocaust* (New York, 1982); Karl A. Schleunes, *The Twisted Road to Auschwitz. Nazi Policy Toward German Jews, 1933-1939* (Urbana, 1970); Christopher Browning, *Ordinary Men. Reserve Police Battalion /OJ and the Final Solution in Poland* (New York, 1992); Richard Breitman, *The Architect of Genocide. Himmler and the Final Solution* (New York, 1991); Omar Bartov, *Hitler's Army. Soldiers, Nazis, and War in the Third Reich* (Oxford, 1991).
[3] Ruth Bettina Bim, "Revising the Holocaust,: in: *The Historical Journal*, 40, 1(1997), pp. 195.215; Norman G. Finkelstein, "Daniel Jonah Goldhagen's 'Crazy' Thesis: A critique of *Hitler's Willing Executioners*," in: *New Left Review*, 224, (July/August) 1997, pp. 39-87.

action that has already had a chilling effect on his critics.[4]

Why have scholars been so critical of Goldhagen? First, he claims that he is the first person to work in court records. This is so patently false as to be embarrassing, for scholars from Gitta Sereny in her work on Franz Stangl[5] in the sixties to Browning in the nineties, have worked in German court records from the trials of war criminals in Germany.

Second, Goldhagen claims to be the first to recognize the true nature of German anti-Semitism, a strain of anti-Semitism so virulent as to call for the elimination of all Jews from Germany. According to Goldhagen this "eliminationist" anti-Semitism can be traced in Germany all the way back to the earliest medieval times and had by the 19th century captured virtually every facet of German intellectual and cultural life.

Further, Goldhagen claims to have developed what he calls a "cognitive model" of German behavior, according to which every German action with respect of the Jews was motivated by "eliminationist anti-Semitism."

> The Holocaust was a sui generis event that has a historically specific explanation. The explanation specifies the enabling conditions created by the long-incubating, pervasive, virulent, racist, eliminationist anti-Semitism of German culture, which was mobilized by a criminal regime beholden to an eliminationist, genocidal ideology, and which was given shape and energized by a leader, Hitler, who was adored by the vast majority of the German people, a leader who was known to be committed wholeheartedly to the unfolding, brutal eliminationist program. During the Nazi period, the eliminationist anti-Semitism provided the motivating source for the German leadership and for rank-and-file Germans to kill Jews. It also was the motivational source of other non-killing actions of the perpetrators that were integral to the Holocaust.[6]

For Goldhagen, "eliminationist anti-Semitism" was an autonomous actor on the historical stage, "shaping Germans' actions," virtually bewitching the Germans in their hatred of Jews and their violent, murderous actions:

---
4 *Der Spiegel*, 49, 1997
5 Gitta Sereny, *Into That Darkness* (London, 1974).
6 Goldhagen, p.419.

> The autonomous power of the eliminationist anti-Semitism, once given free rein, to shape the Germans' actions, to induce Germans voluntarily on their own initiative to act barbarously towards Jews, was such that Germans who were not even formally engaged in the persecution and extermination of the Jews routinely assaulted Jews physically, not to mention verbally...
> ...Once activated, Germans' profound hatred of Jews, which had in the 1930's by necessity lain relatively dormant, so possessed them that it appeared to exude from their every pore....[7]

The implications of this notion are particularly vexing on two levels: first, if "eliminationist anti-Semitism" was this powerful an actor how are we to apportion individual responsibility among the perpetrators? And, second, what, then, is the actual role of Adolf Hitler? For "eliminationist anti-Semitism," according to Goldhagen, seems so well-established and so powerful even before the rise of Hitler that the Fuhrer is reduced to nothing more than the tool of the more powerful forces of history. Oh, by the way, in case any of you might have forgotten, that is *precisely* how Hitler described himself in *Mein Kampf* and from the podium: "I carry out the commands the Providence has laid upon me," Hitler often proclaimed to his audience. And once the war began, a war, as we all clearly understand, against the Jews as well as nations, he assured his people: "No power on earth can shake the German Reich now, Divine Providence has willed it that I carry through the fulfillment of the Germanic task." [8]

Tragically, few of Germany's Jews who lived through the Thirties under Hitler are still alive. Hence, it is unlikely that Goldhagen's arguments—central among them that all Germans were innately, and murderously, anti-Semitic—might be challenged by a Jewish survivor of those perilous times. Dr. Frank Wesley is such a man, whose actual experience living under Hitler gives him a unique perspective on Goldhagen's thesis. Wesley takes on Goldhagen head-on. Wesley gives his readers a brisk tour of medieval and early-modern Jewish life in Europe, demonstrating with elegant clarity that anti-Semitism was no greater in Germany than in the rest of Europe. Indeed, he points out, Jews fared worse

---
7 ibid. p. 449.
8 Walter C. Langer, *The Mind of Adolf Hitler. The Secret Wartime Report* (New York, 1972), p. 36

in medieval England than in Germany in the Middle Ages. He illustrates the participation of Jews in Germany's unification, and the cooperation at the university level, especially in science and medicine, between Jews and Gentiles in Wilhelmine Germany. Dr. Wesley's account takes on an immediacy as he moves his reader into the Weimar Republic, drawing upon his own experiences as a student in the Twenties.

Often, as Dr. Wesley summons up his own past, the reader is reminded that his are the details Goldhagen has chosen to leave out. Even as Goldhagen consciously leaps over the Weimar period in his narrative, completely ignoring the Twenties, Wesley reminds us that for "…Jews, like myself, who received their public schooling in the Weimar Republic [the Twenties], had reached the zenith of the Jewish-German symbiosis." [9] With the eye of one who would later become a psychologist, Wesley observed Germany's descent under Hitler.

And he cautions his readers, not every German hated Jews. Indeed, many were simply indifferent. Arrested after *Kristallnacht* in November 1938, Wesley recalled being rounded up in his native Breslau: "As we Jews were driven through the streets of Breslau at night, the bullhorns and the torches signaled our approach. Windows opened in the tenement houses on both sides of the streets. There were no boos and no cheers. Just silence. As our column came closer many windows were closed and the curtains drawn." [10]

For me, as an historian of the Holocaust, the power of Frank Wesley's essay comes from two quite distinct sources. First and foremost, this is a statement of personal experience. And this *personal* experience is tempered by the psychologist's understanding of human nature and human behavior. Second, this is a work based entirely on sources available to Daniel Goldhagen. Frank Wesley is not a trained historian. Nevertheless, using materials, *all* of which were published *before* Goldhagen's book appeared and thus available to Goldhagen, Frank Wesley paints for us a more nuanced, and consequently more useful, picture of anti-Semitism and of Germany's treatment of the Jews under Hitler.

---

9 pp. 20-21 in draft.
10 p. 41 in draft.

Introduction

As thousands of Jews were driven through the streets of Breslau, few of us knew that we were on our way to Buchenwald. The bullhorns blared, "Keep walking you murderers!" Some of us were beaten bloody with swagger sticks and rifle butts. We thought the SS had gone temporarily mad, but still believed that there would be justice at our place of destination, wherever that would be.

In 1938, we Jews had already lived under Hitler for almost six years. We knew Dachau had been established in 1933, but hardly any of us knew that Buchenwald existed and that about 7,000 Gentiles and 1,000 Jews were already behind its electric fence. The vast majority of Jews, German Gentiles, and foreign diplomats did not know that four large concentration camps with thousands of inmates were already in operation a year before Hitler invaded Poland. Moreover, what was not known and imaginable at the time was the daily routine in the camps, the murderous working conditions, the brutal beatings, and the gruesome floggings.

I am writing this book in response to Daniel Goldhagen's work, *The Holocaust: Hitler's Willing Executioners*, in which he presents the average German as innately anti-Semitic, merely waiting for Hitler's signal to brutalize the Jews. Part I deals with the history of anti-Semitism showing that there was no more anti-Semitism in Germany than in any other European country and that in the 19th century it was pronounced in Russia where Czar Alexander III was advised to let one-third of the Jews emigrate, one-third convert and one-third die of hunger.

Part I also discusses the loss of World War I, economic conditions, and the growth of the Communist Party—non-antisemitic factors which propelled Hitler to power. It is shown that the votes for Hitler rose and fell in relation to Germany's unemployment, a fact which contradicts Goldhagen's assumption that the German's anti-Semitism was latent until Hitler encouraged and rewarded it.

Several chapters in Part I deal with the conditioning of anti-Semitism, the staged demonstrations against the Jews, the indoctrination of the Hitler Youth, and the training of the concentration camp guards. Collectively, they show that the brutalities in the camps were perpetrated by specially trained and select groups whose leaders, vying for Hitler's favor, devised the most brutal and gruesome ways of torturing and killing millions of Jews, Russians and Poles.

The brutalities which the camp guards inflicted on their non-Jewish victims, and the atrocities committed by the Rumanians and other non-Germans against the Jews are also discussed, facts which suggest that the causes of brutality are poorly understood and that it is an oversimplification to attribute them solely to an innate Germanic anti-Semitism.

During the 12 years the Nazis were in power persecuting and killing the Jews, the Germans never helped the Jews in any organized way. Goldhagen considers this lack of assistance a major proof for the existence of a deep-seated anti-Semitism within the ordinary German. In Part II it is pointed out that the Jews did not feel threatened during Hitler's rise to power and saw no need to establish an active defense of their own. Once Hitler came to power and Jews were being arrested and mistreated, the need for outside help became urgent. As soon as Hitler was given emergency power, he destroyed the leadership of his opposition parties: the Communists and the Social Democrats, factions which might have furnished organized rescue units.

Part II also describes the treachery by which Hitler obtained his dictatorial powers which enabled him to crush almost all of his opposition in practically a single night. The secrets which surrounded the early "Protective Custody" arrests, as well as the entire concentration camp operations, are enumerated to show that any rescue attempt was bound to fail. The misinformation which the Jews were given all along their path of destruction deterred them from revolting, obviating the need for any Gentile group to come to their aid. In the few instances where the Jews did receive a modicum of help from the Polish and the Czech underground, they suffered devastating reprisals. When Heydrich, the Jews' worst enemy, was shot, Himmler had 5,000 Czechs, Jews and Gentiles shot to revenge his death.

I hope that this book will clarify some of the sources which lead to the Holocaust and that it will heighten our attention towards the growth of dictatorships. The realization that the destruction of the Jews was concerted by Hitler and his trustees, not by the public at large, should not lessen our future vigilance. Minorities are in danger of destruction when hatred against them developed over centuries, but they are in an even greater danger if their destruction can be instilled in a people in just one decade.

THE HOLOCAUST AND ANTI-SEMITISM

Part 1
Anti-Semitism in Germany

Chapter One

Anti-Semitism in the Middle Ages

In view of the fact that millions of Jews were systematically tortured to death at the hands of Germans, it is plausible to assume that most Germans were violently anti-Semitic. Yet the historians disagree in their assessment of anti-Semitism in Germany. Some believe that Adolf Hitler was responsible for the of the Jews and that the Holocaust would not have happened without his paranoid rage. Other historians maintain that the anti-Semitism of the Germans helped Hitler to expedite his annihilations, and still others, like Goldhagen, maintain that Hitler could have never carried out his massive execution plans without the anti-Semitism which was deeply ingrained in the average German.

In the following, it will be shown that anti-Semitism during the Middle Ages was no more pronounced in the German lands than in other European countries. It will also be discussed that for three generations before Hitler came to power, Gentiles and Jews had lived peacefully in Germany and that their conjoint efforts contributed much to the emancipation of the oppressed and to the era of enlightenment in politics and theology.

The Jews settled in Germany as tradesmen and craftsmen in the wake of the Roman legions. Their first tragic phase began in 1096 when they were massacred by the crusaders. The crusaders began their pilgrimage in France aiming to destroy the Moslems in the Holy Land. As they gained momentum moving through the lower Rhine region and along the Danube, they burned Jewish settlements and tortured and killed those who would not become Christians. In the following centuries, the Jews had a turbulent existence throughout Europe. At certain times and localities they were free to travel, were granted protection, and were given certain privileges and concessions. At other times, they were restricted in their movements, put into ghettos, heavily taxed, forbidden to marry, plundered, tortured and killed.

Though Goldhagen presents the "Jewish Problem" as an indigenous German one, the facts show it started in Rome and was present in all European countries. Several popes had ruled that the Jews must serve Christians for not having accepted Christ, as formalized by the Decretal of Innocent III in his "perpetua servitus" in 1205. In France and in Germany, various ecclesiastical and secular rulers often disagreed about the meaning of "eternal service" – whom and how the Jews should serve. In England, where the authority was more centralized, Edward the Confessor had ruled in 1135 that the Jews were to serve the King only (servi camere regis). He decreed that they were free to travel, pay taxes only to him, and that harming a Jew would be like harming the King's property. Though the Jews could not be harmed by others, they could be killed or banned from England only by the King's command as it finally happened in 1290.

Goldhagen points to the many ritual murder accusations and the subsequent pogroms which occurred in Germany. Referring to the German people, he states: "the will to kill was...embedded deep in their belief about the Jews." However, as documented by Langmuir (1990), the first recorded accusation of ritual murder occurred in Norwich, England around 1150. Thomas of Manmoth generated the account of the "Boy William" to show that the Jews still crucify Christians in order to insult Christ and to acquire blood for their own rituals. Later, around 1200, the Abbot of Saint-Mont-Michel recorded that the Jews had crucified "Young Richard" at Pontoise. England acquired its most famous mythical victim in 1155 with the death of "Hugh of Lincoln." Henry III, King of England, investigated this alleged crucifixion fantasy, that the Jews kill Christians for ritual cannibalism, and had 19 Jews executed. This was the first execution of Jews ordered by a major authority. Hugh was enshrined as a saint in the Lincoln Cathedral. By the middle of the 13th century, England had four such shrines established for the alleged victims of ritual murders.

Concerning the ritual trial in modern Germany, Goldhagen (p.64) cites Pulzer (1964) and Sterling (1969) who reported that 12 ritual trials took place in Germany and Austria between 1867 and 1914, and that even the liberal newspapers treated the ritual murder charges as proven facts. This, however, is a one-sided account as there is evidence in newspaper and court records that justice did prevail in the trial in Xanten in 1891-92 where even the public prosecutor pleaded for acquittal and the accused Jews were exonerated. There was also the trial in Konitz in 1900 where the witnesses were convicted of perjury, and where the editor of an anti-Semitic newspaper was jailed for slander against the tribunal personnel. (Adler, 1969).

In France and in Germany, the treatment of the Jews in the 13th and 14th centuries was not as unified as in England. Jews, when mistreated or persecuted in one principality, could not even move to a neighboring one. There was a number of synods and conferences, attempts to regulate the status of the French Jews, the so-called "non-retention agreements." In 1223, Louis VIII was able to get an agreement from 25 lords that Jews who moved into their principalities should be seized and returned to their previous domicile.

In spite of these attempts to regulate the lives of the Jews and in spite of the Papal bulls (Gregory the Great, Gregory IX, and Innocent IV) which decreed repeatedly that Jews should not be harmed, massacres did occur in France. The Count of Blois, for example, had 32 Jews killed in 1171 to avenge the alleged death of a single child, where the corpus delecti could never be found. Another major massacre occurred in Valreas in 1247. The chimeral fantasies that Jews drink Christian blood for medicinal purposes and that they kill Christian children to show their contempt for Christianity had apparently spread to France. Though Frederick the II and several popes had forbidden the propagation of the "Blood Libel" accusations, the sporadic killing of Jews continued until the Jews were expelled from all of France in 1394.

The Jews were never totally expelled from Germany, though at different times they were banned from certain lands and from city-states. The first major recorded massacre occurred in the city of Fulda in 1235 where the Jews were accused of having caused the deaths of three children who burned in a fire on a Sunday morning while their parents were in church. The most serious and widespread persecutions in Germany occurred about a hundred years later in 1349, when hundreds of Jews were killed in Frankfurt, Nurnberg, Mainz and other cities. This wave of killings followed the declaration of Charles IV who authorized local rulers to kill their Jews as long as they compensate their King for it. The motives for killing the Jews in Germany – financial greed and religious Judeophobia – were the same ones for which the Jews had been killed in England and France. Yet the Jews in Germany suffered throughout the entire Middle Ages because they were never fully banned from the German lands as they were from England in 1290 and from France in 1394. Moreover, there was more opportunity in Germany to persecute the Jews because when they were driven from one area, they were often accepted, if not invited, in a neighboring state.

After a generation or two, they would often be persecuted in this new state, and at times they were even readmitted to their original locality. Vincent Fettmilch and his followers, for example, plundered the Frankfurt Jews and drove them out of the ghetto in 1614, but the ruler of the neighboring city of Mainz sent boats to rescue them. He also sent soldiers to have Fettmilch and his ringleaders hung and ordered the magistrate of the city of Frankfurt to pay restitution. (Kracauer, 1925).

In the theological sphere, the Jews received similar treatment. Luther, for example, claimed in 1523 that the Jews had every right to reject the Papist Christianity and maintained that he would have done likewise had he been a Jew. But twenty years later in 1543, when he found out that the Jews did not convert to Lutheranism as he had hoped for, he published his book, *The Jews and Their Lies*, in which he called the Jews "Disgusting vermin whose synagogues are devils' nests of insolence and lies..., thirsty bloodhounds and murderous of all Christendom... together with the lowliest serfs, the Jews should be locked up in barns and burned." (Luther, 1523, 1543). (At the Nurnberg Trials, Julius Streicher tried to defend himself claiming that the murder of Jews was not his own but Luther's command)

Luther's teaching caused the expulsion of Jews from various German cities, but they were again readmitted and given special privileges during the Counter-reformation period when the bishops regained some of their power. Ironically, the Jews received their greatest help from the staunch Lutheran King, Gustavos Adolphus. Though he did not allow Jews to settle in his own Baltic kingdom, he granted them certain privileges in his conquered territories. While his soldiers committed horrible atrocities against the German Catholics, they had orders not to pillage or disrupt the Jewish population. The Swedish Army commanders found the Jews to be efficient suppliers for their quartermasters, paying them for their services in favors, concessions, and protection. Some of these favored Jews, the "Court Jews," became influential in the governments of various principalities in the 17th and 18th centuries. Goldhagen traces the roots of the Holocaust back to the persecutions and killings the Jews suffered in the German lands during the Middles Ages. He sees in these persecutions a rather harsh and brutal 'Germanic' type of anti-Semitism and he believes that it became embedded into the German culture, implying the Jungian concept of the 'collective-folk-conscious.' Yet, even a cursory look at the anti-Semitism during the Middle Ages shows that the motives for banning or killing the Jews – religious fanaticism, mythical fears, and economic greed – were the same in all countries.

Chapter Two

Pre-Nazi Anti-Semitism

When assessing the degree of anti-Semitism in Germany in the 19th century, Goldhagen presents few comparative data. Of all European countries, Russia was by far the most anti-Semitic (Marrus, 1987: Schapiro, 1978). Dostoevsky wrote openly that the Jew was a harmful and alien element in the Orthodox community. The pogroms of 1881, the expelling of the Jews from Moscow ten years later, and the government-sponsored destruction of hundreds of Jewish settlements in 1905 shocked the entire civilized world. (Ettinger, 1978). In contrast, the German Jews during this time were protected by the law and had equal rights. In conjunction with the German Welfare Office and their own Jewish Aid Society (Hilfsverein der deutschen Juden), they were able to shelter the hundreds of Russian Jews who arrived daily at the train stations in Posen, Breslau, and Berlin. From 1905 to 1914, the Jewish Aid Society was able to relocate 700,000 refugees, providing half of them with passage to America. (Rinott, 1976).

Goldhagen also fails to discuss the anti-Semitism in France which became pronounced during the latter half of the 19th century. When the province of Alsace was annexed to Germany in 1871, its citizens had the option to choose their nationality, and most Jews opted for German citizenship. There were riots against the Jews in Paris during the Dreyfus Affair and the Panama Crisis when the government was reluctant to protect the Jews. Theodor Herzl covered these events as a reporter for a Viennese newspaper. While observing the intense hatred of the French toward the Jews, he came to his final conclusion that the Jews must have their own homeland, and that the assimilation which he advocated in his earlier years was bound to fail. Citing more than a dozen German anti-Semitic authors, Goldhagen maintains that the

"Jewish Problem" received more emphasis in Germany than in other European countries. But the theological literature in general dealing with anti- as well as pro-Jewish issues was also more abundant in Germany. Due to the age of reason, advances in science, and Marxism, religious values were questioned on all fronts. Surely, the German anti-Semites were not the only ones who wrote about the "Jewish Problem" or the "Jewish Question" (Judenfrage). In the 1870's, Jewish scholars in Russia began to question the value of life in diaspora (Schachtman, 1978). While the Russian Jews had a problem of not being accepted, some German Jews felt that their own assimilation had gone too far and that the German Jews were losing their religious identity due to the increasing number of mixed marriages and their disregard for their religious rites. (Scholom, 1979).

In relation to their own assimilation, the German Jews experienced another problem – the influx of Eastern Jews (Ostjuden). Fleeing the pogrom and the Russian war machine, the number of Eastern Jews in Germany began to equal that of the German Jews. Most of the German Jews had a strong disdain for the Eastern Jews who wore dark clothes, had long beards, and were very direct and forceful in their business interactions. In what was called "Semitic anti-Semitism" (*Deutsche Wochenschrift*, 1885), the German Jews felt, wrongly or rightly, that the Eastern Jews' demeanor would evoke the stereotypical anti-Semitism of past centuries. Even Theodor Herzl, when still a student at the University of Vienna, felt that the Eastern Jew "lacked character," and insisted that these "foreign" Jews intermarry and observe a common state religion [Catholicism] (Bain, 1940). Another assimilated German Jew, Heinrich Friedjung (1885), editor of a German weekly referred to the Eastern Jews as the "tenacious and alien part of the population."

A voluminous literature ensued, written mostly by the Jews, dealing with the question as to whether the Eastern Jews should assimilate or preserve their own orthodoxy while living in Germany. The German, Jewish philosopher, Hermann Cohen, believed that Reformed Judaism, a product of German-Jewish assimilation, is a free and powerful religiosity in harmony with the culture of the respective country. It brings advancement to orthodoxy, a proof against unbelief and ethical skepticism, and is a rejoinder against the redemption-belief of Christology. Publishing in the same journal, *Der Jude*, other German Jews (Landauer, Buber, Blumenfeld) argued that it was Cohen's own insecurity which made him overestimate the value and the depth of his assimilated Reform Judaism (Gilman, 1979).

Both Jews and Gentiles saw problems in the Judeo-Christian assimilation. Some Christian theologians, not necessarily anti-Semites, were likewise concerned about the religious liberalism of the German Jews. They feared it may spread to the Gentiles, making them less religious. Other Gentiles had practical and political concerns. The respected historian, Heinrich Treitschke, demanded in 1880 that the Jews convert to Christianity in order to become social and cultural equals. If that could not be obtained, he believed, they would be better off living in their own country. About the same time, the court preacher, Adolf Stocker, declared that the Jewish Question, for him, is not racial or religious, but rather a social-ethical one, unless the Jews convert to Christianity. Stocker founded the anti-Semitic Christian Socialist Party.

In 1890, Stocker joined with several small anti-Semitic parties to form the "Anti-Semitic League." This party never had more than 250,000 members receiving no more than half a percent of all popular votes. Though the members were few, some of them tried to incite provocations between Jews and Gentiles in the rural areas by making false accusations. To combat this trend, representatives of the German Jews met several times in Berlin during the 1890's to plan a defense against slanderous anti-Semitic accusations. It was suggested that the Emperor be petitioned to outlaw anti-Semitic slander, but the majority of the representatives felt that this was unnecessary, since the Jews, like any other citizens, were already fully protected under the existing law. Even after Hitler proclaimed the Nurnberg Laws, most of us Jews felt that our basic human rights were still guaranteed as long as we followed the law. We believed this until thousands of us were on our way to Buchenwald.

Chapter Three

The Symbiosis

Goldhagen enumerates the anti-Semitic events which occurred in pre-Nazi Germany, but the interactions between Jews and Gentiles can be more fully understood by considering additionally the many positive relationships which existed during that same period. Admitting that it may sound paradoxical, Bieber (1979) believes that the Jews never had such an intimate and reciprocally satisfying relationship with any other people in modern times as they had with the Germans during the Kaiser Reich and the Weimar Republic.

The granting of civil liberty and religious freedom can be traced back to the emancipation literature of Moses Mendelsohn and Ephraim Lessing, a Jew and a Gentile. Mendelsohn interpreted the Pentateuch from Hebrew into German and maintained in his philosophical writings that there is no conflict in being a German and also a Jew. He became friends with the classicist Lessing whose plays deal with the tragic contradictions caused by nationalism, classes and religion. In his most popular play, *Nathan the Wise*, Lessing shows that unity can be obtained when prejudice is overcome. Lessing's works were seminal for Goethe and Schiller who wrote about humanism and the equality of men.

Schiller's early tragedies are attacks upon political oppression and tyranny caused by social convention. His works were translated into both Hebrew and Yiddish and served as a symbol of freedom to many oppressed Russian and Ukrainian Jews. Niewyk (1980), reviewing the cultural history of the German Jews, points out that in the Enlightenment, furthered by Kant, Goethe, and Schiller, were the highest expressions of German culture and in no way distinguishable from the essential quality of Jewish ethics. There was a special kinship between Judaism and German humanism. As the Jews were given egalitarian rights, the Gentiles of all classes were also granted equal rights mainly through land and tax reforms advocated by Stein, Hardenberg, and Humboldt.

Politically, the Jews were as involved in the Kaiser Reich as were the Gentiles. It was Edward von Simpson, a converted Jew, who offered the crown to the King of Prussia when he became Emperor (Kaiser) of Germany in 1871. Two Jews, Eduard Lasker (1829-1884) and Ludwig Bamberger (1823-1899) were leaders in the National-Liberation-Party and became Bismarck's coalition partners. In 1880, they influenced Bismarck to give the Labor Union a legal status to oversee workmen's compensation laws, health insurance, old-age and disability benefits. This was the first time in the world that social benefits were given a legal status.

The architect of the German labor movement had been another Jew, Ferdinand Lassalle (1825-1864). In 1863, he became the first elected president of Germany's Labor Union. He thought it would be to every government's advantage to adopt social legislation in the form of minimum wage, health insurance, and fair labor practices. When the German Reich was founded, several other Jews made important contributions to her legal system, notably Paul Leband, who authored the German constitution and Levin Goldschmidt, who formalized the German commercial law. Goldschmidt became a federal judge and, in 1872, became the first non-converted Jew appointed to a university professorship.

The above mentioned Jews, along with the leaders of the National Liberation Party: Lassalle, Riesser and others, were elected by Gentiles in spite of the fact that they were running against Gentiles. That they were Jews did not deter the majority of Germans to vote for them. Anti-Semitism was apparently not as widespread in the Kaiser Reich as Goldhagen portrays. Goldhagen's hypothesis that anti-Semitism was 'latent' at these times is likewise untenable since a small group of politicians and theologians kept anti-Semitism vivid enough to be a conscious factor in the decision making process.

At the turn of the century, many important discoveries were made at the German universities, some being the product of a conjoint effort of Gentile and Jew. Heinrich Herz, for example, who discovered the short waves, was a student of Hermann von Helmholtz. The synthetic production of nitrogen was discovered by the Jew, Fritz Haber, and the Gentile, Carl Bosch, for which they were awarded a joint Nobel Prize in 1918. A further example is the discovery of nuclear fission by the Gentile, Otto Hahn and the Jewess, Lise Meitner. Numerous other examples of collaborative efforts in the humanities and sciences are given by Kaznelson (1962) who cites the work of 4,000 Jews who made outstanding contributions to the arts and sciences.

The German public schools were multi-denominational. Protestant, Catholic, and Jewish students received the same instructions, except for one or two hours per week of religious studies when they went into separate classrooms to be instructed by their respective clergy. In the average school class, the amount of students were approximately fifteen Protestants, ten Catholics and three or four Jews. I never felt odd or singled out for these religious instructions, since the majority of the students, the Gentiles, were also separated. In my ten years of public schooling, I cannot recall any incidents of having been insulted or beaten up because I was a Jew. The most serious fights during the final years of the Weimar Republic were between Protestants and those who were in Communist and Nazi youth organizations. Most of our friendships were formed among those who lived close to each other and those who had common extracurricular interests such as chess, radio, language clubs, etc. Religion was not a dominant criterion. The Jews, like myself, who received their public schooling in the Weimar Republic, had reached the zenith of the Jewish-German symbiosis. Most of our parents and grandparents had attended public schools and we received our 'German' values both at home and in school. Furthermore, our practice of 'Reform Judaism' made our lifestyle practically indistinguishable from the way Gentiles lived.

Reformed Judaism was in itself a by-product of the German-Jewish assimilation. In the climate of European emancipation, Jewish scholars followed the dictum of Moses Mendelsohn, who wrote in 1780 that a Jew can also be a German. They began to re-examine the Pentateuch and the Talmud to search for a form of worship which would maintain their basic monotheistic values without requiring the observance of the Mosaic food laws , the daily usage of phylactery, the wearing of the yarmulke, etc. The first rabbinical seminar was established in the city of Breslau in 1854, where less ritualistic and mythological approaches to Judaism were being formalized. Students from other countries came to Breslau and to other seminars in Frankfurt and Berlin, where they were introduced to more liberal forms of Judaism. Reformed Judaism became firmly established in Germany. Its crowning symbol was the New Synagogue in Berlin, which the Reformed Congregation dedicated in 1866. It was the largest synagogue in the world with a seating capacity of 3,000 and a gilded cupola 150 feet high.

In the second half of the 19th century, the German culture was looked upon favorably in much of the world and the ideals of the acculturated German-Jewish community became those which would dominate worldwide Jewry (Schwarzchild, 1979). While the German-Jewish symbiosis has left few offspring and little of its culture in present-day Germany, Reformed Judaism, which has become the Jews' dominant form of worship throughout the world, is perhaps the greatest legacy the German-Jewish symbiosis has left behind.

Chapter Four

Hitler's Anti-Semitism

There was nothing specifically German about Hitler's anti-Semitism. It had two main thrusts--a racial and an economic one. The racism which Hitler followed was already outlined in 1859 by the French Count, Joseph de Gobineau. In his book, *The Inequality of the Races*, Gobineau ranks various races and categorizes the Black Africans as the least and the white Aryan as the most advanced race. Hitler came in close contact with Gobineau's ideas through the British-born Houston Stewart Chamberlain (1855-1927) who was Richard Wagner's son-in-law. Chamberlain wrote in 1906 that all great cultural accomplishments were of Germanic origin and that the non-Germanic races, particularly the Jews, infect these accomplishments. They mix with Germans while keeping their own race pure and spotless. In order to assure that Germans survive, wrote Chamberlain, it is their duty to free themselves of Jewish blood. Hitler followed Chamberlain's suggestions very faithfully.

As expressed in hundreds of speeches, Hitler's second major motive for hating the Jews was his fear that "International Judaism" would rule the world through capitalism and also through communism. This illogical contradiction was already advanced by Henry Ford at the beginning of World War I. Ford blamed the international Jewish bankers for starting World War I and for fomenting the Russian Revolution. To disseminate his anti-Semitism, he bought the *Dearborn Independent* and began accusing the Jews in weekly editorials for America's past and present misfortunes: for Benedict Arnold, the Civil War, Lincoln's assassination, etc. What the Jews could not achieve by money, media or manipulation, he wrote, they would achieve by pandering to the sexual perversions of the powerful and prominent (Black, 1984).

Ford's collected editorials were published in Germany under the title, *The Eternal Jew*, under the authorship of "Heinrich Ford" in 1923. Hitler's *Mein Kampf*, which he wrote a year later was similar to Ford's ideology and contained passages taken verbatim from Ford. In 1930, after Hitler's party had become successful, Hitler admitted to a *Detroit News* reporter that he regarded Henry Ford as his inspiration. Once Hitler came to power in 1933, millions of Ford's books were distributed to schools and party offices throughout Germany.

The combined fears of Jewish world domination and a consequent impurification of the Aryan race gave Hitler's anti-Semitism a paranoid urgency – a mission to destroy the Jews and to save the Aryan race and the world. Hitler's anti-Semitism was global and he was seeking a global cure.

Hitler did not only hate the Jews, but also all other non-Germanic races, most of all the Jews and the Gypsies because they were non-Aryans living within Germany. Before Hitler came to power he did not publicly mention his contempt for the Slavic races. But during the war years, in the early 1940's, he and his staff made elaborate plans to put all Poles and Russians into servitude, if not slavery, once the war was won. They specified that the Slavs would only go to school until their twelfth year to learn a minimum of reading and writing not to exceed 500 words, but a maximum of obedience and servitude to the German super race. This subjugation was already practiced in the occupied Polish territories. Polish women and children above the age of 10 were sent as virtual slaves to work on German farms. Younger children with Aryan features were often taken away from their Polish parents and sent to German families to be raised as Aryans (Remak, 1969).

Hitler also hated the Black races. In discussing racial purity in *Mein Kampf* in 1926, he wrote: "While our European people fall into physical and moral leprosy, the pious missionaries wander to central Africa and establish Negro missions to turn healthy though inferior children into a foul breed of bastards...our future State will prevent this permanent degradation and beget images of the Lord and not deformities of half man and half ape."

The very 'Christ killer' motive which Goldhagen identifies as the root of German anti-Semitism is totally absent in Hitler's hatred. To the contrary, Hitler hated everything Christian and he hated Judaism for having been the source of Christianity. In his nightly "tea talks," he said that Christianity was a hoax engineered by the Jews to throw off their Roman yoke. He mentioned that Christ was actually the son of a whore and a Roman soldier and that the lie about his divinity was spread by Paulus-Saulus. Hitler mentioned that if he would have had a choice he would have preferred to live in Roman times since the Romans were still free of society's two greatest evils--syphilis and Christianity. He frequently told his inner circle that the public is too naive to accept the truth, and that a belief in dogma is necessary for striving towards greater unselfish goals (Heins, H. 1980).

Hitler had no Christian values. He was devoid of any humanitarian feelings or forgiveness. He interpreted 'Social Darwinism' to give him the right, if not the duty, to kill the weaker species, race or person. He would give orders to kill Jews, Poles, Russians, German communists, as well as his closest Nazi associates, without regrets. A year after he became Reichschancellor, he had the leader of the Brown Shirts, Ernst Roehm, and his entire staff killed within one day. Suggesting a meeting with Roehm and his staff to discuss their differences, Hitler arrived at night, awoke Roehm with the words, "you are under arrest," and had him and about 100 other high-ranking Nazis shot the next day. These killings occurred without warnings, accusations, trial and evidence. Hitler, Himmler and Goering had made a hit list a week or so before the night of the 'Long Knife', as it became known afterwards.

While the direction of Hitler's anti-Semitism came from outside sources, the intensity with which he pursued it was his own. There has been much speculation about the ferocious driving force behind Hitler's hatred of the Jews. His rejection by the Viennese Art Academy has often been cited as the source of his anti-Semitism, though several acquaintances reported that he was not preoccupied with anti-Semitism during the five years he lived in Vienna from 1908 to 1913. They reported that he was a loner and had no close friends in the house for unemployed men in which he stayed. He painted postcards which two of his house mates sold for him. He felt comfortable with both these men, with the Gentile, Hanisch, and the Jew, Neumann. He also sent respectful 'Thank You' notes to his family physician, Dr. Bloch, the lawyer, Dr. Feingold, and the picture framer, Morgenstern. All three were Jews and had encouraged him by buying his watercolors. (Fest, 1974).

In *Mein Kampf* (p. 56), Hitler describes that he began to hate Jews gradually when he saw swarms of them in Vienna's Inner City who did not resemble Germans, who were physically and morally repulsive, and who did not fit the rest of humanity. He mentions that it became an obsession with him imagining that Jews, in long caftans and black hair, were invading every aspect of the German culture.

Hitler wrote *Mein Kampf* about 10 years after his Vienna days and it is likely that he sanitized the onset of his anti-Semitism. There are reports from his Viennese cronies that he attempted once to seduce a blond model but was prevented by a half-Jewish rival. While these reports are dubious, it becomes obvious that he had a pathological fixation on the sexual relationship between Jews and Gentiles. His speeches and his writings are full of passages like: "the repulsive bandy-legged Jewish bastard wants to seduce blonde girls...with satanic joy the black-haired Jew lurks in wait for the unsuspecting girl whom he wants to defile with his blood." When Hitler decreed the Nurnberg Laws in 1935, he set one of the heaviest punishments for any liaison between Jew and Gentile. For Rassenschande (race-defilation), the Jew could get a death sentence and the Gentile, a life-long concentration camp sentence.

Reports from his psychiatrist, Dr. Krueger, (1943) point likewise to a racially motivated sexual obsession. Hitler told Dr. Krueger that his first attraction was to a brunette whom he met in a cafe in Vienna. But the first time she invited him to visit her home, her father threw him out, telling him that his daughter could never have a Gentile boyfriend. Hitler also mentioned another occasion when a Jewish brunette hit him in the face when he was trying to seduce her. Hitler left, but returned later with some of his cronies who gang-raped her while he watched standing in attention and beat her after the ordeal. Hitler was well capable of revenge. Because he knew too much, Hitler had his former Viennese house mate, Reinhold Hanisch, murdered soon after the Annexation of Austria – 25 years after he had last seen him.

It is questionable whether psychoanalytic reports represent reality. But the mere frequency and the vehemence with which Hitler mentioned Jewish women suggests a strong emotional involvement. By the time he contacted Dr. Krueger in the early 1920's, his fear of Jews had turned into a systematized paranoid delusion. He insisted that a Jewish Army doctor had injected him with syphilis even though his tests had turned out negative (Krueger, 1943).

There were a number of incongruities in Hitler's past which could have given rise to several inferiority complexes. Hitler adored blond Aryans, yet he had dark hair. He was Austrian, but longed to be German. He was a draft-dodger in Austria and moved to Germany to avoid the draft. In Munich, he registered as "stateless" to foil a possible extradition. But a year later he readily joined the German Army and became a very calm and fearless soldier.

Whatever Hitler's internal motivations and his anti-Semitic feelings were, he remained politically inactive, until he attended a meeting of a small nationalistic, anti-capitalistic and anti-Semitic group, called the German Worker's Party, headed by Anton Drexler, a railroad machinist. During a discussion (not about Jews, but about the cessation of Bavaria), Hitler spoke publicly for the first time, forcefully and emotionally for 30 minutes. Recognizing Hitler's oratory skills , Drexler invited him to join his party, handing him a membership card, No. 555. After thinking it over for two days, Hitler joined as board member No. 7, in charge of recruitment and propaganda. Hitler wrote that this was the most decisive resolve of his life. From this day on, in 1919, there was no turning back (Hitler, 1943, p.224).

After Hitler found his mission he changed the Party's name and took over its leadership. He gave hour-long speeches full of anti-Semitic invectives accusing the Jews of being "bloodthirsty and avaricious tyrants, glorifying fratricide, manipulating the Bolshevists, Freemasons, capitalists, and Jesuits. In his talks, Hitler seemed to be feeding his own paranoia. His insults grew worse the longer and louder he talked, ending up by calling the Jews, "the creeping venom of society, the syphyllizers of our race [he often made up his own disparaging words], pestulous boils, adders devouring our nation, pussy abscesses which must be lacerated, etc."

It is now almost unthinkable that most German Jews, including myself, were not upset hearing some of Hitler's speeches. Though it is difficult to be objective after knowing that the Holocaust fulfilled every bit of Hitler's anti-Semitic fantasies, I must admit that few of us worried about our future when listening to Hitler. One had the feeling of watching the development of a psychosis, somewhat like listening to an anti-Semitic rap artist without taking the content of his drumming rhythm personally.

There were also some objective reasons for our calm and complacency. Hitler was considered a 'Gutter' anti-Semite and those before him had never been successful, though no one had been as vicious as Hitler. Furthermore, as already discussed, for the first eight years, from 1919 to 1927, his party was losing votes, falling to about 2%. Even when Hitler was gaining votes in the early 1930's, we still did not become alarmed. Perhaps we had become accustomed to his diatribe , believing words have always been cheaper than deeds. We still felt safe even after Hitler was appointed chancellor. Two-thirds of the Germans were still solidly against Hitler. The officer corps disliked him because he was not of the aristocratic class and he was not a German. He had no ally among foreign nations; even Mussolini had referred to him as the "Hun up North."

Some opposition leaders even welcomed Hitler's appointment to the chancellor office. The Vice-Chancellor V. Papen said "now we have him roped in," and the speaker of the Social Democratic Party, Rudolf Breitscheid, clapped his hands anticipating that Hitler would soon ruin himself since he could never get two-thirds of the legislators to agree with him. A month later, however, Breitscheid was taken into custody.

A year later, two generals were assassinated, Papen's office was abolished and two of his aides killed. Several years later, Breitscheid died of torture in Buchenwald (See: Part II, Crushing the Opposition).

Chapter Five

Voting for Hitler

In order to understand the makings of the Holocaust, it is necessary to examine the factors which motivated the Germans to vote for Hitler. Most historians agree that various adverse conditions in the Weimar Republic brought Hitler an overwhelming number of votes (Marrus, 1989). Goldhagen, in contrast, is one of the few writers who hypothesized that a special brand of German anti-Semitism was the main driving force for Hitler's success. In the following, however, it will be shown that Hitler's anti-communist and anti-Versailles platform catapulted him to power and that his anti-Semitic tirades had little effect on the number of votes he received.

As Goldhagen points out, Hitler's earliest speeches already contained some of his most vile attacks on the Jews. In the years following World War I, from 1919 to 1924, his party gained steadily, reaching finally 6.5% of the popular votes in 1924. These years were times of great turmoil in Germany, of unprecedented inflation, severe food shortages, and a number of communist uprisings. In 1924, the currency began to stabilize, Germany had been accepted into the League of Nations, and a rapprochement between France and Germany took place. Within the next four years, the "Golden Years," Germany's national income rose 12% above its pre-war level and unemployment fell to an all-time low, less than 2%. Concurrently, with the improvement in the economy, the votes for Hitler fell from 6.5% to 2.6%. During those four years, from 1924 to 1928, the public showed practically no interest in Nazism, in spite of the 2400 party demonstrations held throughout a single year, the year of 1925. This disinterest is also reflected by the sale of Hitler's book, *Mein Kampf*, which sold 10,000 copies in 1925, but only 3,000 in 1928 (Fest, 1974 p.251).

As the world economic crisis and the depression years began, around 1928, Hitler's party experienced a sudden increase. It received 18% of the votes in 1930. As the depression worsened, and unemployment rose in Germany from half a million to six million within a few years, the Nazi Party rose likewise to an all-time high in July of 1932, receiving 37.3% of the votes. Within the same year, there was another striking correlation between unemployment and votes for Hitler. Franz von Papen, a member of the Central Catholic Party, who was Reichschancellor during 1932, was able to obtain a 3-year moratorium on Germany's war debts. Monies were reallocated to certain Public Work Projects which reduced unemployment by about one million by the end of 1932. Simultaneously, Hitler's party lost about a million votes, obtaining only 33.1% of the votes in November, which was the second election during 1932. Percentage-wise, his votes fell from 37.3% to 33.1% within six months (Scheffler, 1964).

Hitler's verbal barrage against the Jews never let up during his 14-year long campaign trail, yet the votes he received fluctuated greatly. If the German people had been overtly anti-Semitic, they would have voted for Hitler in steadily increasing numbers. On the other hand, if their anti-Semitism was latent, as Goldhagen suggests likewise, one must ask why there were two latency periods, or two periods of diminishing votes, one after 1924 and a second one after July 1932. We must ask further which forces turned the latent anti-Semitism into an active one, and vise versa.

As the above has shown, the number of votes Hitler received was related to Germany's economy. As unemployment rose, more workers joined the Communist Party, and as the communist "threat" became greater, more Germans voted for Hitler. From the five major parties which existed in the Weimar Republic, Hitler's party was communism's fiercest opponent. For years and in almost all of his speeches, Hitler had consistently warned his audiences of the "Red squads of butchers...the bloody morass of bolshevism...who had slaughtered millions of their own people and had drowned thousands of German prisoners-of-war in the Neva...etc." He repeatedly urged his listeners to join his party to prevent that Russia's fate would not become Germany's. (Baynes, Vol. 1, 1942).

Many Germans voted for Hitler to safeguard against a communist victory and a possible Soviet Union takeover. Soon after World War I, there had been several communist takeover attempts;

one by the Spartacists in 1918 when thousands of workers declared the City of Berlin a communist territory, and another one in 1919 when Kurt Eisler declared Bavaria a Communist Republic. In Hungary, Bela Kun had actually established a dictatorship of the proletariat. Many Germans who voted for Hitler did so because they feared the communists and not because they feared the Jews.

The fear of communism helped Hitler in two ways. It brought him votes and it brought him money. The votes came from the large conservative middle class who feared Soviet atheism. His money came from several industrialists like Kirdorf, Thyssen, from the wealthy publisher Hugenberg, who all feared the loss of their wealth. They provided Hitler with practically unlimited funds. With these monies, Hitler put on the greatest "media blitz" in the history of democracies. He salaried leading party members, paid others to attend rallies, and provided fancy uniforms, weapons and medals for his followers. Furthermore, party headquarters (Braune Haus), were established in all major cities as well as training camps for Pre-Hitler Youth (Jungvolk), the Hitler Youth, and the German Girls (BDM). A variety of sports clubs were founded; the National-Socialist Automobile Club, a Flying Club, etc., with the party supplying campgrounds and equipment. In the intellectual sphere, the Nazis financed university fraternities and set up their own "Speakers Academies," where they trained political agitators in public speaking. In the critical election year in 1931-32, over 2,000 "graduates" were added to their propaganda machine.

To attract the masses, Hitler used public address systems, which were a novelty at the time; light shows, fireworks, torch parades at night, and colorful flag and banner parades during the daytime. He and his entourage drove the latest and most expensive Mercedes cars. In one week before an important election, Hitler spoke in 21 towns, addressing as many as 100,000 people in a single day. The visual aspects alone made his rallies especially appealing to the younger generation. As a 13-year old, I felt a curious attraction to all this fanfare and with an older cousin of mine I went to one of these mass meetings held in the Sports Stadium in Breslau. There were gigantic fireworks and rows of searchlights creating a light wall reaching into the sky. In comparison, the rallies of the Social Democrats which I often attended, seemed very drab.

It is questionable whether and to what degree, Hitler's hate propaganda influenced the German adults. It did, however, greatly influence the younger generation. In youth camps and at sports events, the Jew was constantly portrayed as the villain. The youngsters were taught such hate songs as "when Jew blood squirts from our knives we can stab twice as deep." They were conditioned to hate the "Jew" in the symbolic sense. Most of them had probably never met a Jew, and would not have recognized one if they had. There were several judicial attempts to ban the teaching of hatred and killing, but Hitler always hid behind the "Free Speech" clause guaranteed by the Weimar Constitution–the very constitution Hitler was aiming to destroy. The Hitler Youth members furnished the very first concentration camp guards (see: Conditioned Brutalities).

The threat of a communist takeover was greatly magnified by Hitler. The Communist Party never became more than the third ranking party in the Weimar Republic. Its members, the Red-Front Fighters, however, were the ones who provided the main physical opposition against the Nazis. They fought them in the beer halls and in the streets. (Members of the Social Democrats, the Reichsbanner, would also fight the Nazis, but to a lesser extent). In the early Munich days, the communists would attend Nazi gatherings trying to break them up by shouting and throwing beer bottles and other objects. The Brown Shirts were originally founded to protect the Nazi meetings against infiltrators. But as the Nazi party grew in numbers, the Brown Shirts became the more frequent agitators. The Nazis wanted to show the public that the communists are out to destroy capitalism and, in one incident, while not in uniform, they smashed up merchandise in a department store. (Hilberg, 1967).

Whether the communist threat was real or imagined, the frequent street fights between the Nazis and the communists became a great annoyance, if not a public danger. There were sudden incidents in the streets in which attackers would step out of a building hitting or shooting an unexpecting victim. Within moments the fight was over with the attackers disappearing and the victim left wounded or dead on the sidewalk. On one May-Day, several clashes in Berlin resulted in 19 deaths and 30 severely injured persons (Roegner, 1958). The police arrested several hundred members of both parties. Hitler always cried foul play. In Berlin, he claimed that his "innocent" party members were arrested because the Berlin Chief of Police was a Jew. Hitler also used the confrontations with the communists for his propaganda. He brought some of his severely wounded men to the speakers platform while accusing the communists and the Jews of murdering and injuring law-abiding Germans. Up to Hitler's takeover in 1933, there had been 40,000 trials meting out a total of 140,000 years of imprisonment for murder and bodily injury to members of both parties (Fest, 1974). After Hitler came to power, all Nazis serving prison terms were released, while all non-Nazis were sent to concentration camps.

While the fear of communism was the major reason Germans voted for Hitler, their dislike of the Versailles Treaty provided an additional reason. Most Germans, regardless of their political persuasion or their religious affiliations, considered this treaty oppressive. It required Germany to pay heavy reparations to the Allies which its ailing economy could not afford. At one instance when the Weimar Government defaulted, the French reoccupied the Saarland, confiscated cattle from farmers and coal from the mining companies and transported both to France. This left a very bad taste with the German populations. Hence the abrogation of the Versailles Treaty was one of Hitler's strong propaganda points. Hitler promised, if elected, he would immediately stop all reparation payments to foreign nations. He also advocated the retaking of the territories Germany had given up after losing World War I. He went even further, with the promise of a "Greater" German Reich. As with most of his election promises, Hitler did not elaborate how he was going to accomplish the gaining of (the new) "Great" territories. Few Germans would have voted for Hitler had they known millions of them would die in his attempt to conquer Russia.

Chapter Six

Staged Anti-Semitism

Hitler had paranoid fears that the Jews intended to destroy Germany and had a burning desire to destroy them first. Barely in power for a month, he planned a week-long boycott of all Jewish businesses to begin on April 1st, 1933.

When the news of the planned boycott reached the foreign press, various Jewish organizations, labor leaders, and members of the clergy began to stage anti-fascist demonstrations in New York, London, and other major cities. They demonstrated against the import of German goods. Fearing an immediate financial ruin of the newly founded Nazi state, almost all of Hitler's friends and closest advisors urged him to call off his planned boycott.

For days Hitler refused until a plan was devised (probably by Goebbels who spent hours with him in Berchdesgarden on March 26th) to portray the boycott as a defensive action against the "atrocity lies" the Jews were spreading abroad. The boycott would also be portrayed as a preemptive strike against further agitations by the Jews in New York and London where mass demonstrations were in the planning stage. Hence, the Nazis planned to call off the boycott at 7 p.m. on its first day and grant a three-day pause until the following Wednesday in order to give the Jews abroad a chance to cancel their anti-German demonstrations. If the Jews refused, then the boycott in Germany would be resumed with full force.

The German papers revealed these boycott plans in detail on March 28th. Dr. Goebbels gave a radio address on the day before the boycott, reemphasizing that the boycott was a defense against the World Jewry which threatens the livelihood of German workers. He ordered his Brown Shirts to be posted outside the Jewish stores and commanded them not to harm anyone and to prevent any violence the public might carry out against the Jews on that day.

On the morning of the boycott, my father and I took the streetcar to our downtown business. Judging from the passengers' behavior, it seemed to be a normal Saturday until we came to the inner-city where the Brown Shirts were stationed in front of many stores. Some showcase windows were defaced with large stars of David and with the words "Don't Buy From Jews." The passengers in the streetcar became restless. Some expressed their disgust in audible tones, commenting: "What a shame," "How unjust", etc. My father and I were silent. We already knew some Jews had received threats for making anti-fascist remarks. The Gentiles, apparently, had not received such threats. Some of them still said what they thought.

Most of the Gentiles kept on buying at "Jewish" stores. They were not deterred even though some Brown Shirts took their pictures and threatened to put them on a black list. Some Gentile customers phoned my father on the boycott day to express their regrets and to offer their continued support. Barkai (1989) describes other accounts where Gentiles–specifically on this day–went to Jewish stores and Jewish doctors to express their loyalties.

The boycott was over in a day. It was Hitler's first official action against the Jews and he was successful on several accounts. The Jews inside Germany were fooled into believing that they were still comparatively safe from physical harm. Secondly, he had the Germans believe that he was not aggressive, but was merely defending himself for the good of the German worker and storekeeper. Furthermore, he convinced part of the world and some future historians (as e.g., Goldhagen) that it was the desire of the average German to destroy the Jews economically, and moreover, that he was the ameliorating influence in this struggle.

As later described in detail by Black (1984), the German public did not know that Goering had ordered five prominent Jewish leaders to travel immediately to England to urge their co-religionists there and in the U.S., to stop all ongoing and future anti-German demonstrations. He added that the failure of their mission would have dire consequences for all the Jews still left in Germany. Under this threat, the anti-German demonstrations abroad abated and the German import-export business went back to normal, giving the Nazis several more years to build up their army and navy.

Another publicly staged anti-Semitic "show" took place one month later on the 1st of May. Wearing their Nazi uniforms, university students combed the library collecting tons of books written by Jews, Communists, Socialists, and others who did not agree with the Nazi ideology. In Berlin, about 20,000 books were taken to a main public square, the Opera Plaza, where Goebbels addressed the public during a burning ceremony.

This spectacular event caused many unfavorable editorials in the foreign press, particularly in America and Britain. But as before, Hitler operated under the motto that attack is the best defense. Directing himself to America, he said in his speeches that America, of all countries, had the least reason to complain about Germany's (Hitler's) plan to separate the Aryan from the Jewish race, because American immigration laws had long excluded certain races of which Americans disapproved. He added that the Jews in Germany had not suffered one iota of discomfort. Addressing himself to England, Hitler mentioned that England, in spite of her vast colonial territories (Lebensraum), did not allow anyone to enter unless they could bring lots of money along. Germany, on the other hand, had allowed penniless Jews to enter from the East for decades, and therefore, suffered great food shortages. "If England is so concerned about the German Jews," Hitler asked, "why doesn't England allow them to enter without bringing thousands of dollars along?" (Baynes, 1942).

Despite the staged anti-Semitic demonstrations and the constant anti-Semitic propaganda through the radio and the press, which were solely under the control of Hitler's Propaganda Ministry, the relationship between Jews and Gentiles had not changed significantly. My Gentile school friends still visited me, especially those whose parents had belonged to the Socialist or Communist parties. My mother, who had been dismissed from her university position, was still invited by her former Gentile colleagues to join discussion groups in their private homes.

Two years after Hitler came to power, the public was still not rejecting the Jews. Our separation needed to be dictated. Hence, in a totally unexpected move, Hitler announced the "Nurnberg Laws" at the Reichsparteitag in 1935. Jews were declared "second-class citizens". Any liaison between a Jew and a Gentile was suddenly punishable for both with perhaps a life-time sentence. This law came as a complete surprise to Jews, Gentiles, and the world at large. Again to lessen the reaction of the foreign press, Hitler announced further that the laws were not intended to persecute the Jews, but merely to equalize the economic conditions within Germany. He said that the Jews had enriched themselves at the cost of the German people, and that the new laws are only correcting a past injustice.

After, the Nurnberg Laws' restrictions multiplied by about 200 more in the next few years. Some were ridiculously detailed; for instance: Jews were not allowed to salute the Swastika; Jews could not employ female Gentiles under 45 years of age; Jews could not use certain trains, seats, toilets; etc. Other restrictions had grave economic consequences, such as: Jewish doctors could no longer treat Gentile patients; Jewish lawyers could no longer represent clients in court; and later on, Jews could not practice any profession which required a state license. As our gainful employment became restricted, our social interaction with Gentiles became likewise much reduced. Jewish pupils were expelled from all public schools and we were not allowed to enter theaters, dances or any other social gatherings where Gentiles were present. (Krausnick, 1965).

The Nazi government did allow us to establish our own schools, especially technical schools where trades such as gardening, agriculture, and mechanics were taught and were considered useful for the purpose of emigration. The government also allowed us to set up our own theaters, the Kulturbund, where there were excellent performances, lectures, and social gatherings. All programs, actors, and lecturers, however, had to be previously approved by the Nazis' Ministry of Culture (Freeden, 1964).

In spite of the years of progressively restrictive anti-Jewish legislation, there had never been a public outcry or a pogrom-like action in the six years Hitler had been in power. The Gentile public did not follow the suggested assaults propagandized daily through the radio or the press by Hitler, Goebbels, and others.

But to make their prophecy come true and to show the world that the German public was against the Jews, Goebbels staged the Crystal Night. (The Nazi leaders vied with each other to persecute the Jews to please Hitler. The Crystal Night was apparently planned by Goebbels. Hitler and Goering were actually annoyed when it happened.)

To make the public outcry more believable, the Crystal Night was staged on the day after the death of von dem Rath, a German consular officer in Paris, who was shot by a Jew. Goebbels ordered the Gestapo to arrest as many male Jews as they could find in public places and in Jewish homes at night. He also ordered all synagogues to be set on fire. When the synagogue in Breslau began to burn, the fire engine arrived, but they were ordered not to extinguish fire but only to stand by to protect the neighboring buildings.

While the synagogues were burning and the first Jews were marched to the railheads, Goebbels announced in a special night broadcast that the German people had started to riot against the Jews to avenge the death of von dem Rath. He announced further, that he had ordered all rioting to be stopped, and that a special tax will be levied against the Jews (Suhnesteuer) as the Jews would have to pay for the broken showcase windows and for cleaning up the rubble which was left of their synagogues. That was Goebbels' official announcement. In reality, the arrests continued several days until almost 20% of all Jewish males in Germany were behind barbed wire.

As on previous occasions, the Nazis pretended that it was the desire of the German public to harm the Jews and that the Gestapo had to intercede to protect the Jews and take us into "protective custody" (Schutzhaft). But the Nazis were never successful in inciting any public action against us. It was not the German public but the uniformed SS who marched Jews to the railheads and beat those of us who could not walk fast enough.

Goldhagen has commented on the mass arrests during the Crystal Night. He assumes that the Gestapo would not have been able to arrest 30,000 Jews during one night without a large number of civilians showing them where the Jews lived. Goldhagen considers this supposition as another proof that anti-Semitism was "deep-seated" and widespread among the German public. However, this supposition is not warranted since the Gestapo had access to the local police registers and did not need any outside informants. In Germany, as in most other European countries, a person's religion was an integral part of all identification papers. Any change of domicile had to be registered with the nearest police precinct. Lists of members of certain religions, professions, age groups, etc., were always readily available. The Gestapo did not need the German public to point the finger at the Jews.

As we Jews were driven through the streets of Breslau at night, the bullhorns and the torches signaled our approach. Windows opened in the tenement houses on both sides of the street. There were no boos and no cheers. Just silence. As our column came closer, many windows were closed and the curtains drawn.

Chapter Seven

Conditioned Anti-Semitism

In the last free election in the Weimar Republic, Hitler received one-third of the votes. Most of the remaining votes went to parties opposed to Hitler's politics. Why were most Germans not willing to vote for Hitler in 1932, when seven years later, they were willing to be his "willing executioners," as Goldhagen asserts. Goldhagen attributes this willingness to a culturally inherited anti-Semitism which was latent until Hitler or Heydrich gave the command to kill. In the following it will be described how Hitler and his propaganda minister, Dr. Goebbels, after having obtained dictatorial powers, used the most intensive conditioning procedures to train segments of the population to kill on command.

Hitler had gained votes by making the public fearful of communism and he continued this tactic after he became chancellor. Barely a month in office, he staged the Reichstags (Parliament Building) Fire, claiming that a communist revolution had started it. Fearing the communists, President Hindenburg granted Hitler his request for emergency powers to suppress the communist plot. With this totally unexpected move, Hitler was able to occupy the headquarters of his opposition parties and arrest most of their leaders, causing a total disarray among his opposition forces in practically a single night (See: Part II–Crushing the Opposition).

Hitler had the mandate to prevent a communist plot but the order he and Goering, his Minister of Interior, gave the police units read: "...arrest mainly communists, but also those who cooperate with the communists to further their criminal aims, and also those who support them indirectly..." (Reichstagsbrandverodnung, March 3, 1933). The Jews were not mentioned in this order; neither the Social Democrats, nor the Catholics. The Nazi Party did not yet have the majority in Parliament and President Hindenburg could have rescinded Hitler's emergency powers. (Hindenburg had been the presidential candidate of the Social Democrats and beat Hitler in the previous year, 1932, by six million votes.) Although the arrest decree mentioned only communists, by adding the words 'support' and 'indirect' the Nazis made it appear legal to arrest anyone, Jew or Gentile, whomever they disliked. Within the following months c50,000 Germans, Gentiles and Jews were arrested and put in make-shift (Wildcat) camps where some of them were tortured to death (Broszat, 1965). Most of these arrest occurred in secret, without warrant, with the arrestee held incommunicado, and without right to counsel.

Though Hitler had successfully eliminated all organized resistance and had absolute dictatorial powers by 1934, he continued his unrelenting hate campaign against the Jews and the Bolshevists. He had a vision of the Great German Reich which entailed conquering the Russians and making them German vassals. Hitler's major conditioning method was that of "successive approximation,"reaching his aim by small increments. Publicly, for example, he would only reveal a small part of his plans. In the above mentioned arrests, e.g., he only mentioned the communists, but arrested also Social Democrats, members of the clergy, etc. Hitler also used "successive approximation" when spreading hatred against the Jews. At the beginning, his verbal attacks were directed against specific groups such as the Jewish Bolshevists or the Jewish bankers. Later, he included all Eastern Jews who lived in Germany and finally, he attacked all Jews living in Germany.

The legal restrictions against us were likewise decreed in small increments. In education, for example, the Jews were first expelled from the Universities; a year or so later they were forbidden to attend high school; still later, this extended to middle and trade schools. Finally after the Nurnberg Laws, all Jewish children had to attend private Jewish schools. This gradual restriction process occurred over a three-year period. The professional restrictions came likewise in small dosages. The Nurnberg Laws of 1935 restricted the professional Jews, comprised mostly of medical doctors and lawyers. These laws were followed by six addenda with the last one issued in 1938. Each addendum narrowed the Jews' professional practices. Jewish doctors, for instance, were first dismissed from government hospitals. Later, they were no longer reimbursed by the National Health Insurance for their services, and still later they were not allowed to practice in any private hospital except in the Jewish hospitals. Sometime thereafter they could no longer treat private Gentile patients. In the end, they could no longer call themselves "doctors" and could only function as "nurses" (Krankenpfleger) assisting Gentile doctors. Other professions were restricted in a similar fashion. New directives were issued about every six months, adding new restrictions upon already existing ones.

The successive approximation procedure worked well for Hitler. Jews and Gentiles were economically separated in rather bearable steps. We Jews still looked healthy, were still well dressed and dared not complain in public. Hence, the Gentiles inside Germany did not feel sorry for us and neither did the outside world. Each restrictive step was too small for any foreign power to come to our aid physically or impose any sanctions against Nazi Germany. (Only after the Crystal Night when 30,000 Jews were marched to the concentration camps, did President Roosevelt recall the American ambassador from Germany, but imposed no sanctions.)

For most Jews, Hitler's gradual persecution had devastating fatal consequences. Many of us became insensitive to Hitler's verbal attacks and accustomed to our financial and social losses. This prevented some of us who did have a chance to emigrate from doing so. Because some Jews, who had resettled in France, England, and Czechoslovakia, had difficulties obtaining work permits, they eventually returned to Germany during 1934-35 . There were also moments when many of us thought that the worst was over. Our false hopes were at times reinforced by the Nazis, when e.g., Goering said that he had nothing against "decent Jews", or when Hitler announced at Nurnberg, after declaring Jews "second-class" citizens, that it should now be possible "to reach a tolerable relationship with the Jewish people." We did not know that he turned to his adjutant and said in private, "...out of the professions into ghettos or territories, where they can do everything as to their manner, while the German people look at them like one looks at wild animals" (Notes from Adjutant, Fritz Wiedemann, 1937).

Hitler was acutely aware of the gradual destruction process by which he conquered most of his enemies. Pertaining to Jews and others, he revealed to his inner circle that he did not want to fight just for the sake of fighting. He then shouted, "I want to destroy him! Then wisdom comes to me and helps me to drive my enemy into a corner where he can no longer stab me. Then I stab him right into the heart" (Broszat, 1965, p.326).

Soon after Hitler came to power the press and the radio were controlled by his newly established Propaganda Ministry. The import of foreign newspapers was restricted and most radios could only receive local stations. Almost every day there were hour-long speeches by Hitler or his ministers in which the word "Jew" was always associated with something evil. Even as late as 1937 when most of the German Jews were already living by the "good graces" of the Gestapo, Hitler did not let up on his attacks. In the closing speech at the Nurnberg Party Day in 1937, he mentioned "Jews" in connection with 'bolshevist' ad nauseum in such phrases as:

> "The Jews carry the torch for the Soviet Revolution...."
> "Jewish agitators drive the Russians to madness...."
> "Jewish minority appropriate to itself all of Russia...."
> "Jewish elements seek to overthrow democracies...."
> "Bolshevist International organized by Jews...."
> "Jewish race rules through brutal dictatorship...."

There were about 20 such comments in a 10 minute section of this hour-long speech (Baynes, 1942, p.698f).

During the early war years and during Hitler's alliance with Stalin, the Nazi propaganda became less anti-Semitic. Germany was winning on all fronts and there was not much for which the Jews could be blamed. But once the German advances in Russia came to a standstill and the Allies began bombing the German cities, the Jew once again became the whipping boy–the object of hatred. Goebbels' propaganda machine proclaimed daily that the American Jews, the World Jewry, and the Bolshevist Jews are responsible for the bombings–the fires in the inner cities, the injured and the dead including women and children. In all the years before the bombings the "Jew" had been associated with the fear of a Bolshevist revolution–an imagined evil. After the bombing, the sufferings were real and the "Jew" was being associated with an experienced evil. This made the conditioning process very effective, serving Hitler in several ways. The hatred against the Jews increased quantitatively and qualitatively in the German population. Secondly, the increased anger was in turn directed toward an increased effort to win the war. Furthermore, it increased Hitler's credibility as he had always prophesied that the "World Jewry is out to destroy Germany."

A decade-long barrage against the Jews, accusing them of the hideous crimes in hundreds of thousands of newspaper articles, placards, and speeches made the German public anti-Semitic. If the Germans had been innately anti-Semitic or if they had a latent tendency to be so, as Goldhagen maintains throughout his book, one must ask again, why did it take such a long and intense conditioning process to make them anti-Semitic? One must ask further whether the Nazis were successful at turning 80%, 50%, or perhaps only 20% of the population into anti-Semitics and whether there were other factors such as the conditioned obedience and the desire for military distinctions which prompted their gruesome acts. Goldhagen does not address these issues. Though he considered certain exemptions, he believes that the vast majority of Germans were anti-Semitic and that this anti-Semitism was the motive for their hideous crimes.

After examining the speeches of Nazi leaders, it appears that even Hitler and Himmler doubted at times the Germans' anti-Semitism. Hitler often reminded those Germans who, for personal or religious reasons, did not accept his anti-Semitism with such phrases as:

> "We must destroy the Jew before he destroys us. It makes no difference whether the individual Jew is decent or not. He will destroy you either consciously or unconsciously. You must not think of it as un-Christian. After all, the Lord our Savior was a fighter who rose to drive the brood of vipers from the temple." (Baynes, Vol. I, 1942).

As late as 1943 in an address to his SS subordinates in Posen, Himmler felt that it was necessary to warn them that some Germans still believe that there are decent Jews. He said: "I am referring to the evacuation of Jews, the annihilation of the Jewish people. This is one of those things easily said: It is our program, elimination of the Jews, annihilation—we will take care of it. And they all come dragging along, 80 million good Germans, and each one has his one decent Jew. Certainly, the others are swine, but this one is an A-1 Jew. Of all those who talk this way, not one has seen it happen, not one has been through it. Most of you know what it means to see hundreds of corpses lie side-by-side, or five hundred, or a thousand. To have stuck this out and, excepting cases of human weakness, to have kept your integrity, this is what has made us hard. In our history, this is an unwritten and never-to-be-written page of glory...." (Dawidowicz, 1975, p. 149).

Not even Himmler who had trained his SS troops to kill Jews and had rewarded them for it, trusted their 'innate' anti-Semitism. After 10 years of Nazism, he still had to give them a pep-talk to continue killing Jews.

Chapter Eight

Conditioned Brutality

The brutalities inflicted on the Jewish camp inmates were rather uniform throughout a variety of factory, work, and annihilation camps. Goldhagen attributes this conformity to a unified hatred, an anti-Semitism ingrained in the German culture. This uniformity, however, can be explained by the common indoctrination experience which began for most guards early in their Hitler Youth training. Beginning in their preadolescence they were conditioned to hate and to kill Jews. They were given daggers with the engraving "Blood and Honor" and they were taught a song with the refrain:

> "when the Jew blood squirts from our knives we can stab twice
> as well–with Jew blood–with Jew blood"

Most guards were conscripted from the Hitler Youth. Once they were selected, they received additional training on how to treat concentration camp inmates. Himmler picked one of the most brutal psychopaths, Theodore Eicke, to set up the training rules for the guards and for punishing and torturing inmates. Through Eicke's rules, millions of people suffered the most unbearable pain and depravation before dying.

Theodore Eicke joined the Nazi Party and the SS in 1928 while working as a security agent for I.G. Farben, Germany's largest chemical concern. He advanced quickly in the ranks of the SS, but fled Germany in 1932 after having been sentenced to a two-year prison term for preparing bomb attacks against the Weimar government. He spent his exile in Italy in an SS camp maintained by the Italian Fascists to give refuge to Nazis wanted by the Weimar Republic.

After Hitler became Chancellor, Eicke returned to Germany. He attacked one of his SS superiors for which he could have been punished by the SS and also by the regular courts. To prevent this, Himmler arrested him first, but sent him for observation to the psychiatric clinic of the University of Wurzburg. While there, Eicke wrote Himmler lengthy letters clamoring for his release. After having been at the psychiatric clinic for three months, Himmler recalled him and appointed him commandant of Dachau in June, 1933. A year later it was Eicke who shot Hitler's rival, Roehm. Just a few days after the Roehm massacre, Eicke became "Inspector of Concentration Camps" and commander of the camp guard units, the "SS Death" formations in 1934.

Eicke set up the following punishment regulations which became the prototype for all future camps. For violating camp regulations, the punishments were: solitary confinement up to 42 days in darkness, with bread and water; and the corporal punishment of 25 strokes with a cane on the bare back. These punishments could be administered separately or in combination. The punishments had to be ordered and executed by the SS personnel. It was specified that caning had to be carried out by several SS guards so that it would be "impersonal" and that it had to be done in the presence of SS guards, the prisoners, and the commander. Milder forms of punishment which could be implemented by the Capos (lead prisoners) were hard labor, dirty labor, drills, beatings, withholding mail and/or food, hard quarters, and tying to posts. For "political offenses"–for talking politics, for gathering with others in order to incite, or for spreading "atrocity propaganda"–there was the death penalty by hanging. To be "shot on the spot" was ordered for assaulting or disobeying a guard, attempting escape, or mutiny.

Eicke also set up the regulations for the selection and the training of the guards. They were to be chosen from members of the Hitler Youth around age 16. They had to receive weekly training sessions first administered by Eicke himself, and later by his cadre. The cadets, and later the full-fledged guards, were constantly reminded that they were special soldiers, that their enemy was not on the front, but behind barbed wire, and must be guarded day and night. They were further indoctrinated by being told repeatedly that they were guarding dangerous enemies of the state, that they must have no pity and obey orders ruthlessly. They must be worthy of the SS and of their special assignment to the Death Head Division—worthy of wearing the skull and crossbones emblem on their uniform.

The guards were also drilled on how to conduct roll calls and on the procedures for marching prisoners to outlying work areas. The guards themselves had to maintain a military posture at all times. They were forbidden to lean against a tree, seek shelter from the rain, or converse with inmates. By 1937, Eicke's guard division had already 5,000 specially trained SS men (Davidovitz, 1975). When the war broke out in 1939, they were already guarding about 100,000 inmates in six concentration and labor camps in stone quarries. In 1942, Eicke and some of his men were called to the Russian front where Eicke was killed. But after his death, his rules and regulations remained essentially in force until the end of the war.

Eicke's regulations were the "official" rules. Unofficially, he promoted only the most brutal guards who had distinguished themselves in their bestiality. Karl Koch, for example, was a master sergeant in the Gestapo Camp, Weserland. While there he chained prisoners around the neck, tying them to dog houses. Like dogs they had to eat out of bowls lapping their food with their tongues. They were ordered to bark when an SS guard approached. Koch would horsewhip or kick them bloody at his whim saying they did not bark soon or loud enough (Hackett, 1995). Eicke appointed Koch as the first Commandant of Buchenwald in 1937. By the end of 1938, Koch had power over the life and death of 20,000 inmates.

In Buchenwald, Koch in turn promoted the most bestial guards to leadership positions. The SS Sergeant, Martin Sommer, for instance, was put in charge of the camp cell blocks, a building with a corridor and two rows of torture chambers. In this rather isolated building, Sommer and his henchmen surpassed all of Eicke's "official" torture rules. They tied piano wires around prisoners wrists and hung them on window bars, so that their feet could not reach the ground. At times they added weights to their feet or swung the prisoners back and forth to inflict more pain. They often added degradation to their tortures like dipping an inmate's face into the feces left unflushed in the SS's toilet before proceeding with Eicke's recommended tree-hangings. They also locked inmates into cells without food or water. At times, death did not come until the tenth day.

For various reasons the guards were at times transferred between camps. Himmler, e.g., ordered Buchenwald's Commandant, Koch, to Lublin to start a new terror camp in Poland. During the last years of the war, the transfer of guards and inmates became more frequent as camps in Poland were being closed and additional ones established in Germany. Like Koch, guards who had distinguished themselves through special efficiency and brutality were often promoted. In Buchenwald, for example, all members of the SS Unit 99 received the Distinguished Military Service Medal for shooting 7,000 Russian prisoners of war within two days.

Considering the official centralized training of the guards, their frequent transfers and the promotions which they were given for their brutalities, it is reasonable to assume that the sadism practiced at the various camps stemmed from their common training and experiences, and not from a common inbred anti-Semitism as Goldhagen asserts.

Chapter Nine

Non-Jewish Victims

Goldhagen sees the camp guards' innate and latent anti-Semitism as the causal factor for the brutality they uniformly practiced in various camps. But factors other than anti-Semitism must be postulated for the brutalities the guards inflicted on non-Jewish victims. Before the war in 1937-38, thousands of German Gentiles, beggars, transients, shirkers, and persons with any kind of police record (from felony to misdemeanor) were sent to concentration or correction camps. Their forced labor was needed to produce bricks and granite stones for Hitler's grandiose building plans.

Once the war started, thousands of Polish resisters and members of the Catholic clergy were arrested and sent to concentration camps in Germany. In his order to arrest the Catholic clergy, Heydrich stated that they are the "sworn enemy" of the Reich and should be arrested without mercy and regard for their rank and that they should be considered for execution if espionage is suspected. After the Russian campaign began in 1941, arrests rose to new heights. Over 15,000 arrests were made alone in the month of October 1941, for example. Half of them were arrested for having quit work. Another category was for forbidden fraternization with Polish prisoners of war. Among those arrested were 80 persons for Catholic resistance, 12 for Protestant opposition and 160 Jews (Table in Broszat, 1965, p. 113).

In almost all camps, the Jews were segregated from the Gentile inmates, but there were also many situations where the Gentiles, especially the Polish resisters, were condemned to hard labor commandos and other deprivations. Whenever these groups were punished, the brutalization they received were, in kind and severity, no different than those inflicted upon the Jews. The Jews, however, suffered more because they had to endure more frequent group reprisals than the Gentile inmates. The additional deprivations which the Jews had to suffer were often administratively devised. In Buchenwald for example, it would be announced: "Thanks to the Jew Rosenfeld, (Roosevelt) who threatened boycotts against Germany, there will be no more food for the day in the Jewish blocks." At times mental torture was added to the physical pain. When the "no-food" day was set for Saturday it would be announced: "On the Sabbath Jews should pray not eat."

Group tortures were not exclusively designed for the Jews. The Jehovah's Witnesses were the first group which collectively suffered degrading and inhuman treatment. By order of the Ministry of Interior, all Jehovah's Witnesses were brought to concentration camps in June 1937. They were called Heaven's Comedians, Bible Worms, Traitors, Dogs of Heaven, etc. Collectively they were assigned to the harshest punishment details. For "special exercise" they were ordered to roll, hop and crawl in the mud while being beaten and kicked. In one instance in Buchenwald, they were ordered to take off all their underclothes and work outside from dusk to dawn in minus 20 degrees (Personal observation; See also: Hackett, 1995).

It seemed that the guards beat the taller and more healthier looking inmates longer and more lustfully. From newly arriving groups, whether Jews or Gentiles, they often picked out the tallest and strongest individuals to be beaten or tortured. Apparently the guards felt more powerful with their sadistic impulses–more satisfied when beating up a stronger, rather than weaker, inmate.

Individuals of the Gentile clergy were often treated as inhumanly as the Jews. When the Pastor Schneider was brought to Buchenwald, he received 25 lashes for not saluting the Nazi flag. He was placed into solitary confinement in a darkened cell and horsewhipped day or night at the whim of the guards. His wounds festered but he was never allowed to bathe. After enduring this torture for 18 months, he was finally killed by lethal injections.

Certain Polish Gentile groups were likewise treated with extreme brutality.

From a group of 181 Poles delivered into Buchenwald in 1939, only half of them were still ambulatory after a four-day ordeal in the stone quarry where they had to run double-time uphill, with heavy loads, through a gauntlet of 10 SS guards beating them with whips and sticks. Once in their barracks in the evenings, the SS guards began to play a cat and mouse game with them. Unannounced, an SS guard would enter the barrack and shout: "Under the table." There was not enough room under the tables and those who were left on the open floor were whipped and kicked, or taken out into the snow for additional exercises and more beatings.

In other instances in Buchenwald, Deputy Commandant Rodl with several of his subordinates would enter the Polish barracks almost daily bringing the "whipping block" along. He pulled out inmates indiscriminately, strapping them to block and whipping them until some of their raw flesh fell off in straps. He administered two or three times more than the 25 lashes, the number which was administratively prescribed.

The guards who tortured Jehovah's Witness, the clergy and the Poles, knew that their victims were Gentiles. The Gentile inmates wore no yellow triangle on their sleeve. Yet the guards went out of their way to inflict upon them their sadistic pleasure beating, or starving thousands of them to death.

It is not known how much sadism depends on genetic or environmental factors. Yet Goldhagen attributes the Nazis' sadism to "structured cognitive forces stemming from a deep-seated anti-Semitism" (p. 409). However, the guards' indiscriminate and haphazard selection of their victims suggests a rather unstructured cognitive framework.

In spite of the inmates' misery or perhaps on account of it, the camps were run in an extremely, if not insanely, orderly fashion. All the physical work, and the bookkeeping was delegated to an echelon of inmates so that the guards had no specific work to do, other than beating and terrorizing the inmates. With whips under their arms, the guards strode from their quarters looking for a reason to beat someone. They usually did not find a reason. Then they would ask the inmates to step out and beat one, or have one beaten by the lead inmate for not removing his cap fast enough when the guard approached. This victim may actually have been the fastest one in removing his cap. The guards may have picked him because he stood first, or last, in line. It was difficult to discern the stimuli for the guards' actions. It would seem that they were driven by an internal desire to beat, yet without having any discrimination, structured ideology or criteria for whom, how, and when to beat.

Chapter Ten

Non-German Brutalities

Goldhagen sees in the brutalities which the Nazi camp guards inflicted upon their Jewish victims a 'deep-seated' anti-Semitism. He believes that the uniformity with which the guards and the killing commandos inflicted their brutalities and the sadistic pleasure they derived from it shows that their will to kill is deeply embedded into their culture (p.163).

Yet, the Holocaust has shown that guards from other non-German cultures killed Jews just as willingly and enthusiastically as their German counterparts.

The Baltic, Croatian, and Ukrainian SS who guarded the ghetto transports and helped round up Jews for open air killings were just as brutal as the German SS. Two days after the killing commando (Einsatzkommando 3) had arrived in Lithuania, the local partisans shot 416 Jews and 47 Jewesses in Kovno. A report from the German commando lists 4,000 Jews who were liquidated 'exclusively by Lithuanians' (Krausnick, 1965).

There were also SS units in Holland and Norway before Hitler invaded these countries. Though their membership was small, they became very powerful once the Germans occupied their country. Yidkum Quisling, the leader of the Norwegian Nazi Party (Nasjonal Samling Party), which had only about 15,000 members before the German invasion, became Prime Minister and a powerful person in the Norwegian puppet regime. The Dutch Nazi Party (Nationaalsocialistische Bewegening, NSB) was likewise very small before Germany invaded Holland. But its 2,000 members were given important governmental positions. A Dutch SS battalion established and guarded the Dutch concentration camps in Assen and Hertogenbosch, and raided the Jewish section of Amsterdam early in 1941, trying to copy the German Crystal Night of November 1938.

Though both the Dutch SS and NSB had few members, they made the resistance efforts of the Dutch extremely dangerous. In spite of this danger and often under the threat of death, the Dutch were able to save about one quarter of their Jewish population from death in Auschwitz (McKale, 1977). Many more could have been saved if the Dutch SS had not arrested Jews and denounced those Gentiles who tried to save them.

By far the worst crimes against the Jews, equal to those of the German SS, were committed by the Rumanian Army. Rumania with about 800,000 Jewish inhabitants had the third largest population of Jews of all European countries. The Rumanians fought with Germany against Russia helping to drive the Red Army all the way back to Stalingrad. The Rumanian soldiers robbed and killed Jews wherever they had a chance on the pretext that the Jews were partisans spying for Russia. After the Rumanian Army captured the Russian port of Odessa, a time bomb exploded in their headquarters killing a number of Rumanian soldiers and several officers. Ion Antonescu, the Rumanian dictator, followed Hitler's model and ordered 100 Jews killed for every Rumanian soldier killed and 200 Jews for every officer. The Rumanians went overboard in their plunderings, beatings, and killings. Within two nights in October about 20,000 Jews were rounded up and marched to the harbor area and shot. Their bodies were covered with gasoline and burned. Other Jews were shot outside the city. Within weeks almost all of the city's 60,000 Jews had been annihilated before the German Killing Commando under the command of Ohlendorf arrived to do the shootings (Reitlinger, 1956).

The Jews in the eastern region of Rumania were considered security risks by Marshal Antonescu, and were driven east across the Dniestr river into Transniestria where the German killing commando (Einsatzgruppe D) was shooting Russian Jews left behind by the retreating Russian army. The killing commando which was moving east consisted of 600 SS men and was 'overworked' and did not want to kill Jews to their front and to their back. Hence they drove the Rumanian Jews back over several Dniestr bridges, but the Rumanians refused to let them re-enter, shot at them and drove them back. This back and forth herding lasted for several days. Thousands of Jews were shot, others died of exhaustion. Even Eichmann complained that the Rumanians should kill their Jews in a more 'planned and slower' way. But Antonescu did not wait.

He ordered Jews into concentration camps where there was no food (Hilberg, 1961).

Inmates in the Pecsara camp had to sell their clothes to the Rumanian soldiers to obtain some food. Most inmates were naked. In other camps inmates were eating grass and cattle food which paralyzed many. The camp Bogdanovka, run by the Rumanian colonel Modest Isopescu, became one of the worst killing centers. After all valuables including all clothing were exchanged for food, the Jews were driven to nearby barns by the thousands, where they were shot and burned. Once there were no barns left, the inmates were marched in groups of 100 to a precipice overhanging the Bug River two miles away from the camp. Before being shot, they had to take off all their clothes and stand naked in temperatures 30 to 40 degrees below zero. Their gold teeth were forcibly taken or beaten out. Those bodies which did not fall into the river were removed by other inmates who were shot after the cleanup.

In his brutal way, Isopescu had massacred about 70,000 Jews; all inmates from the three camps under his command (Bogdanovka, Dumanovka and Akmecetka). (Statistic from Rumanian Peoples court, 1945. Isopescu was condemned to death but was granted an indefinite stay by King Mihai of Rumania.) Under pressure from the German foreign office and the SS, Rumania's Commissar for Jewish Affairs, Minister Radu Lucca, agreed to ship 300,000 Jews to Auschwitz during the summer of 1942. He invited himself to the foreign office in Berlin to discuss transport details. As Marshal Antonescu had already agreed to the deportations, Lucca's visit was considered nonessential by the Germans and consequently he was received only by a party underling. This slight angered him so much that he blocked all deportation of Jews after he returned to Rumania.

In the following year, in 1943, as the Russians began to regain their lost territories, the Rumanians began to fight on the Russian side. Antonescu made a complete turnabout and began protecting all Jews under his domain from further persecutions and the 300,000 Jews slated for Auschwitz survived. It is the largest group of Jews saved by the action of a single individual, by Lucca's vanity, during the entire Nazi reign. It is frightening to realize that Radu Lucca did not save the haunted men, women and children out of any humanitarian feelings, but solely to soothe his ego which had been hurt by a minor Nazi official.

What motivated Antonescu to give the order to destroy Jews and what motivated his soldiers to kill them with such passion and brutality which even dismayed the German killing commandos? Antonescu was in no way beholden to Hitler since twelve of his divisions were fighting with the Germans against Russia.

The reasons why humans dehumanize other humans are not known. The French philosopher, Auguste Comte, postulated a 'contagious mass hypnosis' which may be part of our biological make up. Once a riot or a brutalization starts, others will simply participate without any ideological commitments. There are external factors which incite individuals, groups, and nations to hate and brutalize other religions, races, or nationalities. Only a recognition of these outside variables may improve human relations, while Goldhagen's postulation of an innate factor is not likely to further this aim.

Chapter Eleven

Anti-Semitism Exported

In certain respects Hitler was more successful in exporting his anti-Semitism than spreading it among the German public. After the boycott of the Jewish stores, which the foreign press reported in detail, there were anti-German demonstrations in London and New York. Hitler immediately defended the boycott blaming the Jews outside Germany for it. He claimed that the American and British Jews were trying to boycott German goods and that Germany could only defend herself by boycotting Jewish goods within Germany. He repeatedly warned the foreign countries that they should not fall for this Jewish international conspiracy, lest there would be further and more severe boycotts against the Jews within Germany.

Hitler emphasized repeatedly that the hatred against Germany was spread by "hate mongers," Jewish-Bolshevist fugitives from Germany who wanted to cover up their past misdeeds in Germany, by pulling the present German regime into the mud. To varying degrees, Hitler's propaganda was bought by the U.S. media. For example, the *New York Herald Tribune* wrote that the Jews could prevent the boycott if they ceased spreading "atrocity tales." Similarly, the *Christian Science Monitor* announced that the Nazis were prompted to undertake the boycott as a "rebuke to false propaganda about atrocities" (Lipstad, 1986).

After the annexation (Anschluss) of Austria, Viennese Jews overcrowded the foreign embassies seeking exit visas. To remedy this situation, the U.S. called a conference, the "Nations of Asylum." The representatives of 32 nations met in Evias les Bains to discuss emigration/immigration matters.

America was the first nation which declared through its representative, Myron C. Taylor, that the U.S. did not intend to increase its existing immigration quota of 27,000 per year which included Jews and Gentiles. Most other larger nations follows suit, and did not enlarge their quotas. Canada restricted its immigration to experienced farmers, and Brazil intended to accept only those Jews who had been baptized. Needless to say, few Jews fell into these categories. France refused any help whatsoever. Its representatives stated that Germany had the right to decide what to do with its Jews since they were citizens of Germany. Switzerland complained that about 3,500 Jews were already inside their borders which necessitated an increase in border patrols. Australia declared itself ready to admit 15,000 Jews within the next three years. Nicaragua, Costa Rica, and Honduras refused the immigration of "intellectuals," whatever that meant. Only a handful of the 32 nations present were ready to enlarge their quotas. Ironically, they were Belgium, Holland, and Denmark, the most densely populated countries in the world. The Dominican Republic declared itself ready to accept 100,000 refugees, but there were financial restrictions which few Jews could meet, so that in the final analysis only about 500 Jews were able to go there.

Hitler used the outcome of the "Nations of Asylum" conference to rationalize and "justify" his treatment of the Jews. He ecstatically called America's reaction to his anti-Jewish policy "hypocritical." He said: "It is a shameful spectacle to see how the whole democratic world is oozing sympathy for the poor tormented Jewish people, but remains hard-hearted and obdurate when it comes to helping them." Hitler continued: "We, the democracies (Germany and Italy), cannot *take* the Jews (note the word take instead of keep). We have 135 inhabitants per square kilometer while the Americans and the British and French empires have less than ten." He repeatedly accused the foreign countries of taking the Jews only if they brought money along, which Hitler maintained belonged to Germany, since the Jews got it in Germany. In a talk in Konigsberg (East Prussia), Hitler declared that he would even be willing to send the Jews away with first class tickets on luxury liners if only there would be a country willing to take them (Baynes, 1942). Hitler again turned a defense into an attack.

The conference which was intended to help the Jews helped Hitler to justify his anti-Semitism. It produced no adverse consequences for Germany and it may have encouraged Goebbels to stage the Crystal Night a year later.

Though the events of the Crystal Night were condemned by religious groups, labor unions, and some politicians in several foreign countries, nothing altered Germany's internal policies. Even the recall of the American ambassador did not affect Germany's diplomatic relations with other countries. Scarcely a month after the Crystal Night, Hitler was successful in obtaining a non-aggression treaty with France. It was celebrated with some pomp in Paris and on this occasion the French Foreign Minister, Georges Bonnet, told his German counterpart, von Ribbentrop, not to send any more Jews of which France had more than enough. He also mentioned the French colony of Madagascar as an alternative (Ribbentrop, 1938).

As already mentioned, the most shameful case concerning asylum for the Jews involved the ocean liner, St. Louis, which was turned back by the Republic of Cuba. On board the St. Louis were 917 German Jews who had settled their affairs in Germany and had obtained visas to enter Cuba after having paid the required fees and security deposits. But when the ship reached Havana on May 27, 1939, it was not allowed to dock. While the ship was on her voyage from Hamburg to Havana, the Cuban government, changing its regulations retrospectively, had decided not to accept any more refugees. Cuban navy boats during the day and search lights at night surrounded the St. Louis. Some of its passengers had family members (parents, children, siblings) awaiting them on the dock, but all communications with the passengers were forbidden. A delegation of American lawyers, supported by the Cardinals Spellman and Mundelein, and the president of the United Mine Workers Union, John Lewis, went to Cuba to plead with its president, Laredo Bru. All their efforts were to no avail. After six days of negotiations, the ship was ordered to leave Cuban waters on June 2nd. The next day, the ship's German captain, Gustav Schroder, received orders to return to Germany, but disregarded them by setting course towards South America, and later towards Miami, Florida, where he arrived on June 5th, asking for permission to land. The U.S. Custom Service refused entrance and appeals to President Roosevelt were likewise rejected. On June 6th, the Cuban government showed itself willing again to renew negotiations, being apparently willing to send all the St. Louis passengers to the Isle of Pines if an additional sum of $500 per head could be paid. After an aid committee agreed to this price, Cuba asked for an additional $500,000 but broke off the negotiations before an agreement could be reached. The ship now had more urgent orders to return to Germany. Some passengers committed suicide; many others threatened it. One more attempt was made to land in New York. A philanthropist offered to pay the daily dock fee of $5,000, but Roosevelt still refused to grant asylum. The St. Louis sailed back to Germany on June 8th, after having tried unsuccessfully for 12 days to find refuge for her passengers anywhere in America. Most passengers expected to be sent directly to a concentration camp as had been done with previous "returnees." More suicides occurred. Volunteers formed suicide prevention details visiting cabins periodically. The German captain and the passengers kept on sending pleading telegrams to various heads of governments. When the St. Louis entered European waters, the Dutch agreed to grant asylum to 194 of her passengers, where after England, France, and Belgium agreed that each would take a third of the remainder. It is ironic that both Holland and Belgium, two of the world's most densely populated countries offered asylum, while very thinly populated countries had refused.

The world did not seem to regret the St. Louis incident. Shortly after the ship had returned, England and America sent a joint communique asking Germany not to allow any more immigrants to leave unless they had a valid immigration visa. That was exactly what each St. Louis passenger had, a valid visa to enter Cuba issued by the five Cuban consulates, Cuba's legal representatives in Germany. After the British-American communique, the German government recalled a second "refugee ship" which was already two days at sea. Cuba dealt their refugees an additional ugly blow. Jews who had landed two weeks before the St. Louis' arrival were arrested and sent back to Germany on the Hamburg-America liner, "Orinocco," on July 4th, 1939. As reflected by the news media, the American public was not too sympathetic to the refugee's fate. *The Seattle Times*, for instance, reported on June 5th that Cuba had not invited them (the Jews) and that as harsh as it might seem, President Bru perhaps had no other alternative but to deny them admission. *The Christian Science Monitor* was even more critical, writing that the Jews had no taste for remote and under-developed places, and should remember that other races had carved homes out of wilderness to escape oppression. To a certain degree, the Nazis were successful in exporting their anti-Semitism.

In spite of the many arrests during the Crystal Night and the continued mistreatment of the Jews in Germany, America was not ready to enlarge its immigration quota nor to grant asylum to those Jews who had reached its shores.

Until Hitler attacked Poland in 1939, America had not imposed any sanctions against Germany and the two countries were still cooperating in emigration/immigration matters. For example, in order to grant an immigration visa the American consulates in Germany required that the respective Jew submit a "good conduct" certificate issued by the Nazi police.

On the following page is the author's certificate which his mother obtained from the chief of police for the city of Breslau. It certifies that my behavior was always faultless and that I had never been charged with a misdemeanor or felony.

It is interesting to note that the certificate was issued while I was an inmate in the Buchenwald concentration camp where I was treated worse than any other criminal, receiving neither water nor food for 24 hour periods and being kept for days in an open field in near freezing weather. It was one of the Nazi's propaganda tricks not to call us criminals or felons but to tell the Germans and the world at large that they put us into "Protective Custody" so that the anti-Semitic German public could not harm us.

Der Polizeipräsident　　　　　　　　　　Breslau, den 22. Nov. 1938   193
II 20⁰⁰

Polizeiliches Führungszeugnis

Hierdurch wird bescheinigt, daß __Herr Franz Wolfsohn__
geb. am __15.6.1918__ in __Breslau__ Kreis __stadt__
vom __Geburt__ bis zum heutigen Tage in Breslau _____
gewohnt hat, daß er sich immer einwandfrei betragen hat und nicht für
irgendein Vergehen oder Verbrechen verhaftet oder bestraft worden ist,
mit folgenden Ausnahmen: ---

　　　__2,-__ RM. Gebühren .　　　　　　Jm Auftrage:
~~Gebührenfrei~~

Gültig für Auswanderungszwecke
und gültig für drei Monate, vom Tage
der Ausstellung an gerechnet.

Part II
Why No Help

Chapter Twelve

Jews Were Germans

Because the "final solution" was carried out with unprecedented calculation and brutality, it is generally assumed, retrospectively, that Nazism was a fight between Gentiles and Jews. But in reality the physical battles in the beer halls and in the streets were fought between the Nazis and the Communists—between two predominantly Gentile groups. The Jews fought the Nazis intellectually, mostly through their weekly paper, the *Central Verein*, which was rarely read by non-Jews.

Throughout Hitler's rise to power, the German Jews did not fear him nor his uniformed party members. We felt physically safe since the communists took the brunt of such attacks. We also felt politically safe because in the early 20's the party lost votes, which fell from 6% to 2%. Even after Hitler's party had sudden gains, up to 30%, in the early 1930's most Jews were still not worried. A good majority of Germans still belonged to the opposition parties and there was no indication that the government would ever be toppled (Scheffler, 1964).

There were also some more subtle reasons for our calmness throughout the rise of Nazism which related to our own nationalistic feelings. Most German Jews were proud to be Germans. Compared to the Jews in other countries, the German Jews felt that they lived in a very civil and democratic society, which they had helped to create and to defend in two wars. In our house, for instance, there was a vitrine which contained the Iron Cross my grandfather had earned in the Franco-Prussian War. On another shelf was a picture, shoulder-insignia, and several medals from my uncle, my mother's only brother, who was killed during the Argonne Forest Offensive in 1918.

It was this patriotism which gave many of us Jews the feeling that we were better Germans than the Nazis. Hence, most of us were not afraid of the Nazis, seeing in our own patriotism a certain kind of immunity from any possible attack or persecution. This feeling of immunity was not solely based on wishful thinking. Hitler's anti-Semitic rhetoric was mostly directed towards the Bolshevist and the Eastern Jews who came to Germany fleeing from the Russians and the Poles during and after WWI. Aside from Hitler's more palliative remarks with regard to the German Jews, there was also some action which supported our notion of being somewhat "privileged." Later on in his regime when all Jewish government employees were dismissed, only those who served in the war were allowed to receive their pensions. Even as late as 1938, Jews who had earned the Iron Cross in the First World War were the first group to be released from the Buchenwald Concentration Camp after the mass arrests during the Crystal Night.

Once the war started, the Jewish ex-Army Officers were sent to Theresienstadt (Terezin) which was designed to be a detention rather than a death camp. The few conciliations which Hitler had granted the patriotic Jewish veterans were, as it later became apparent, not for their own benefit. Hitler had to make some of these concessions to pacify some of his own generals who did not approve of the mistreatment of any of their former fellow officers. After the loss of Stalingrad, Hitler lost respect for his own generals. No longer needing their approval, he ordered all inmates, including former Jewish veterans, to be shipped from Theresienstadt to Auschwitz, from detention to death.

Whether our feelings of security and comfort during the years Hitler rose to power were justified or not, the fact remains that there was never any concerted effort on the part of the German Jews to defend themselves. In his account of the Jews in the Weimar Republic, Niewyk (1980) reports only one incident of armed resistance by which the National League of Jewish Frontline Veterans prevented a more serious Nazi attack. This incident occurred on the Jewish New Year in October 1931 when SA men in civilian clothes made hit-and-run attacks on Jews returning from their prayer services in a Berlin synagogue near the Kurfurstendamm. The armed veterans kept the Nazis engaged until the police arrived, making 63 arrests and jailing 20 of the rioters. The Nazi press used this and similar incidents where they had attacked leftists for their own propaganda, claiming that they were attacked first. In the Berlin incident, they blamed the "unjustified arrest" on Berlin's Jewish Chief of Police.

The Jewish Veterans League was founded after WWI in 1919 and had about 30,000 members in the early 1930's. It is reported that the League had clandestine arms caches in Berlin, Munich, Konigsberg, Kassel, and Breslau. They apparently never made any use of these arms as they saw themselves merely as defenders of the Jews, and not as attackers of Nazis. Aside from the Berlin incident, there were no large scale attacks on Jews before Hitler came to power. They were difficult to prosecute since the Nazi attackers were usually in civilian clothes.

There were three major parties in Germany: The Socialist party, the Communist party, and the Central Party. Though they differed in their ideology, they were all much opposed to Hitler and especially to his anti-Semitic platform. But when a new Reichschanceller had to be appointed, these parties were unable to form a coalition. The combination of any two would have sufficed. Politically, the Jews were not a separate entity. The Jewish beliefs were as diverse as the Gentiles' beliefs. Some Jews belonged to the extreme leftists and some were ultra nationalists with the majority spreading their votes among several centrist parties. (There were about five major and 10 minor parties in the Weimar Republic).

The disunity among the general public gave us some security that Nazism would not triumph, while the disunity among ourselves hindered us from creating a stronger self-defense. With the constant political changes, it was not clear who needed help. Hitler took advantage of this division among his opponents and formed a coalition with a smaller Nationalist Party. It gave him a slight majority and he was appointed Chancellor on January 30, 1933. This day was the darkest day in the history of Europe, if not the world. Though we did not know it at the time, within a few weeks it led to Hitler's absolute dictatorship, causing the deaths of millions of Russians, Jews, Poles, and Germans, and of thousands of American and Commonwealth troops defending the free world.

Chapter Thirteen

Crushing the Opposition

Hitler's appointment to the chancellorship did not cause great concern among the Jews. Any law intended to hurt us would still have needed the majority of parliament for enactment, a majority which Hitler, we believed, would never obtain. When Hitler was appointed chancellor, the President also appointed a vice-chancellor, Franz von Papen, a member of the conservative Central Party. The creation of a Vice Chancellory was a first in Germany's history. The president did this to put Hitler in check–a move which gave us Jews and other anti-Hitler groups an additional feeling of security. Our feelings about Hitler's appointment can best be described in Papen's own words, spoken before Hitler's appointment: "We have him (Hitler) roped in. In two months we'll have Hitler pushed into a corner and he can squeal to his heart's content." (Hilderbrand, 1984).

In a totally unexpected move, Hitler crushed all organized opposition in practically a single night. Less than one month after he became chancellor, on the night of February 27th, 1933, Hitler's men, apparently under Goering's direction, set the Reichstags building (parliament), in the center of Berlin, on fire. As the flames shot skyward, which could be seen by the aging President Hindenburg, Hitler proclaimed that a communist revolution had started and asked the president to give him emergency power to deal with this uprising. The president granted this emergency power on February 28th and on this very night, Goering gave the order to arrest all communist and socialist members of parliament, as well as other functionaries.

It is doubtful that the regular police would have arrested members of parliament while they were asleep at home. But ten days before the planned arson, Goering (whom Hitler had appointed Minister of the Interior) had replaced 22 of 32 of Berlin's municipal police commanders with subordinates who were Nazi party members. Moreover, 40,000 SA (Brown Shirts) and SS (Black Shirts) were given auxiliary police power and ordered by Goering to "make ample use of their guns when arresting leftists."

The Nazis first targeted the headquarters and the press offices of the Communist and Socialist parties and of various Jewish organizations. Before the night was over, they had broken into most of these offices, ransacked some of them and occupied others. At the same time, they began arresting leftist leaders at their homes. They now had the membership files and addresses of most of their political opponents, taking 4,000 into custody before dawn. Some prominent Gentile and Jewish politicians were led through the street with such derogatory signs as: "I cheated the public," "I am a Jewish swine", etc. But most of the arrests took place at night or unobtrusively in the streets while a person stepped out of his house or before entering his place of business.

There was utter confusion. Arrests continued for the next few days and even weeks. Nobody knew exactly who was being arrested and where the detainees were. Some who were slated for arrests were able to avoid it by checking into a hotel, boarding a train, or crossing a border. They were mostly forewarned by family members of those who had just been arrested. Hence, if a person did not come home, his next of kin did not know if he was arrested or if he had managed to cross a border. There was a total news blackout about the details of the arrests. The public only knew what Hitler wanted to tell them. In a special broadcast, Hitler announced that through his decisive action he was able to save Germany from communist destruction and that the Reichstags fire was the communists' signal to destroy government buildings throughout Germany.

The question whether or not Hitler's opponents had plans for an organized resistance is inconsequential because Hitler destroyed his enemies before they were able to offer any resistance, literally, while they were asleep. With their leaders arrested, their offices occupied, and their telephone services cut, opposition parties to Hitler ceased to exist. They apparently had no alternative plans to regroup. The caches of guns the Jewish War Veterans were rumored to possess were never used. One of my uncles who belonged to this veteran group received no orders and was unable to contact any of his leaders.

Most Jews heard from relatives or friends of someone who had been arrested but we went to work as usual, trying to hide any fears or anxiety in order to avoid detection by any Nazi who was looking to arrest someone. Some arrests were carried out through the party's chain of command, while others were carried out spontaneously by two or three Brown Shirts. The treatment of the arrestees was likewise very diverse. Several "wildcat" camps established by individual Nazi groups became regular torture chambers. They were located in empty factories or warehouses closed off from public view. Some inmates in these camps were beaten and/or starved to death. Other detainees who were held in the already established penal institutions were treated like regular prison inmates (Broszat, 1965).

It has been estimated that 50,000 persons were arrested in the first few weeks after the Reichstags fire. Half of them were released within a month or so, because there were complaints from German business leaders and from the Minister of Justice, Dr. Guertner, who was a member of Hitler's coalition party and tried to uphold democratic principles.

As the "wildcat" camps were closed, more permanent work and concentration camps were established. In March 1933, Himmler began transferring inmates from the regular Bavarian prisons to empty barracks of an abandoned gunpowder factory near Dachau—Germany's first concentration camp. A few months later began the construction of six more camps in northern Germany.

Individual Jews suffered tortures and degradations and all Jews experienced fears and anxieties during Hitler's first onslaught. But much of this was not known to the public. The Jews were not mentioned in the communications and arrest orders from the Nazis. An order from Goering, for instance, specifies the arrests of communists and their collaborators, anarchists, socialists and anyone who had made derogatory remarks against Hitler.

Likewise, Rudolf Hess (who later became the Deputy Fuhrer) urged his men to kill twelve Marxists for each Brown Shirt who had been killed before the takeover. (Second Brownbook, 1934).

There was a reason why the word "Jew" was not mentioned as the arrest target. Hitler had obtained his emergency power from the President for the explicit purpose to deal with the "communist revolution." Had he mentioned the arrest of Jews, the President might have canceled the emergency power. Hitler never relinquished this power. He waged war, occupied 19 European countries, and had millions killed in camps and on the battle fields—all under the name of fighting communism.

By first arresting those parliament members who were the leaders of the opposition parties, Hitler destroyed the very institutions of the anti-Nazi forces, the forces which Goldhagen blames for not helping the Jews. They ceased to exist before the destruction of Jews began.

It is frightening to read Eicke's (Commander of Dachau) diary and learn that for several months after Dachau was founded, he had only 120 guards at his disposal who had no shotguns and no shells, and only three of these guards knew how to operate a machine gun. (Eicke's Lebenslauf. Instit. Zeitgeschiechte, Fa 74). At this time, perhaps ten commandos could have liberated all of Dachau's inmates. But without a centralized command or a tactical center, such an action was apparently impossible.

Even if some opposition forces had been left intact, they may not have helped the Jews, because the public was informed that the communists and the socialists were being arrested. The Jews were not mentioned. Since the Gentile public could not help the Gentile communists and socialists, it is unreasonable to assume, as Goldhagen does, that they should have helped the Jews.

Chapter Fourteen

Power Through Treachery

Through treachery, Hitler eliminated all opposition inside Germany, inside his party, and inside the continent. He rose to power and maintained it with false promises, assassinations, and misleading propaganda generated by his Propaganda Ministry. After his failed Putsch in 1923, Hitler served only 8 months of a five-year prison sentence by promising to dissolve the Brown Shirts, his strong-arm unit. But he violated this parole condition for which he received an additional assembly and speech injunction. He circumvented this restriction by creating the SS, the storm troopers in Black uniforms, claiming that they were a different organization. He also grouped the SS into 10-men units (Zehnerschaft), each under its own leader.

It has already been pointed out how Hitler falsified his mandate to arrest communists after the Reichstags fire by including Social Democrats, Jews, Freemasons, Jesuits, Jehovah's Witnesses, and others who had never had any connection to the communists.

Hitler's most flagrant act of treachery was the shooting of Ernst Roehm, leader of the Brown Shirts, the Nazis' paramilitary organization, about one million strong. Roehm wanted to integrate his organization with the regular army, but Hitler feared that this would provoke England to declare war, since Germany was restricted to an army of no more than 100,000 men by the Treaty of Versailles. Hitler also feared that Roehm would not obey his orders. Hence, in secrecy with Goering and Himmler, Hitler made up a fictitious hit list pretending that it was secretly obtained from Roehm's headquarters. This hit list contained the names of those high-ranking Nazis whom Hitler wanted on his side.

Hitler waited with his attack until Roehm was vacationing in a resort hotel near Munich. He called Roehm by phone and asked him to invite all of his regional commanders to the resort for a conference, where they could iron out their differences in a "frank discussion" (Roehm thought the phone conversation was amiable). Hitler arrived with about 100 of his elite body guards in the early morning hours the day of the scheduled conference. With two SS men and drawn pistols, Hitler entered Roehm's room and awoke him by shouting, "Roehm, you are under arrest!" In that way, Roehm and his entire staff of about 30 men were arrested and sent to Stadelheim Prison where they were shot the next day. In the north, Himmler and Heydrich had another 50 Brown Shirt leaders shot on the same day.

The treachery and the misinformation went on. The newspapers reported the next morning that Roehm and his staff were executed because they were caught in a homosexual orgy and that Hitler was forced to arrest them to save the honor of his party. Most Germans, including myself, believed this propaganda. We simply had no other clues why Hitler would kill so many of his oldest party comrades, particularly Edmund Heines, the leader of the Silesian Brown Shirts, who was imprisoned with Hitler at Landsberg after the 1923 Beerhall Putsch. Heines was the only leader who was shot in his hotel room because he resisted arrest. He was also the only leader who was caught in *flagrante delicto* with one of his aides. Most Jews in Breslau felt relieved that Heines was killed because he was one of Germany's most cruel Jew and communist haters.

As usual, Hitler was constantly in the public image as the great leader to whom all of Germany pays homage and who was celebrated everywhere. At the time of the pending plot, this media image was greatly elaborated. The night before Hitler planned to arrest Roehm, he was on the Rhine attending a celebration given in his honor. After darkness the Labor Service (Arbeitsdienst) staged a light show for him. On a hillside across from the Rhine, 600 torch carrying workers formed a swastika to honor him. At 4:00 A.M. that very night, Hitler arrived in Munich and was on his way to the Resort Hotel to start the arrests. The day after the arrests, Hitler gave a garden party for important party members at his chancellery in Berlin, where he humored his guests and was attentive to their children; meanwhile, eighty-one of his prisoners at Stadelheim and at Berlin-Lichterfelde were systematically being shot.

Before Roehm was killed, the Black Shirts (SS) were a guard unit within the Brown Shirts and were under Roehm's command. After the Brown Shirt leadership was disseminated, Himmler took on the leadership of the Black Shirts, the SS, which he expanded into his terror organization—an army of ruthless killers running an industrial empire with prison labor, responsible for the death of 12 million civilians and defenseless prisoners.

Hitler's body guards consisted of several hundred specially selected SS men who swore absolute obedience and secrecy to him. On the day Roehm was killed, Hitler ordered several of his guards to assassinate two generals and the staff of his Vice Chancellor von Papen. The murderers were in civilian clothes to avoid a direct connection to Hitler. The SS General, Schleicher, Hitler's predecessor in the Chancellery was shot by a single intruder. A man rang the door bell at Schleicher's villa. When the maid answered, he pushed her to the floor, went into the living room, shot Schleicher at his desk, and Schleicher's wife who was sitting on a nearby sofa.

Hitler did not eliminate all his non-cooperating generals by assassination. He waited, for instance, until his Minister of War, Walter von Blomberg, married a woman of low status. It was alleged that she had been a masseuse in a house of prostitution. To show himself as a populist, Hitler was one of Blomberg's grooms at the wedding. But after some time, Hitler invited Blomberg and told him that the other generals resent him for having married below his class and might not be willing to take orders from him. Hitler urged Blomberg to take a year's leave-of-absence so the rumors would cool down. Hitler suggested that he (Hitler) himself take over the Ministry of War and that in this way, Blomberg would be assured to be reappointed after his year's leave. Hitler, however, kept this ministry for the rest of his life.

General von Fritsch, the Army Chief-of-Staff, was likewise eliminated through a gossip campaign. In his case, it was homosexuality. Alleged witnesses were found and von Fritsch resigned.

In the Reichstags fire arrests in 1933, the Nazis arrested a number of Catholic clergy who had spoken against Hitler or for the Jews. The Pope complained and Hitler, still depending on Italy's and England's graces, backed down and signed the Concordat in July 1933, promising the Vatican not to interfere any longer in the clergy's religious activities. The arrests slowed down for a while, but increased again a few years later. In 1937, the Pope appealed again to Hitler with his "burning apprehension" message. But this time Hitler did not give in. To the contrary, he attacked. In several speeches he proclaimed that the church had no business interfering in the matters of the state.

In his politics, Hitler hardly kept any treaty or promise he ever made. He gave Czechoslovakia an ultimatum to return the Sudetenland, a border strip between Germany and Czechoslovakia. He threatened with total destruction if his demand was not fulfilled. But he also proclaimed in a Sportpalace speech that his request for the Sudetenland, "...is the last territorial claim I have to make in Europe...."

Hitler did get the Sudetenland on October 1st, when he signed the famous Munich agreement,"Peace in our Time",with Chamberlain, Daladier, and Mussolini. Only 21 days later, he assembled his military chiefs ordering them to prepare for the invasion and the total liquidation of the Czech Republic. This actually happened five months later.

In 1939, Hitler began to make demands on Poland for the return of some land from the Polish corridor for a land connection to East Prussia. While the diplomatic negotiations were in progress, Hitler was already briefing his generals for an all out invasion. Moreover, he had made a secret agreement, the "Friendship Pact" with Stalin, his oldest archenemy, who agreed that Russia would attack Poland from the east the day Hitler attacked from the west. Even though he had already set the invasion time for Sept. 1st, 4:45 A.M., he staged a sham Polish attack on a German radio station in the border town of Gleiwitz. At 9:00 P.M. on August 31st, shots were fired and several dead bodies from a nearby concentration camp were left on the scene. This incident was Hitler's pretense that his aggression was merely a defense (Fest, 1974).

In the summer of 1938, several German generals began to organize a plot to remove Hitler and his top SS leaders. When Hitler planned to invade Czechoslovakia, his Chief-of-Staff, General Beck and Field Marshal Braunchtiesch, tried to dissuade him for tactical, and perhaps also, for humanitarian reasons. But Hitler could not be deterred and General Beck resigned, but continued to organize the coup against Hitler. Beck enlisted the cooperation of his successor, General Halder; the Intelligence Chief, Admiral Canaris; the Commander of the Berlin garrison, General von Witzleben, and several other high-ranking officers in key positions. Influential civilians, like the Finance Minister Hjalmar Schacht; the Berlin Police Commissioner, Count Melldorf, and many others were also on the plotter's side. Weapons were distributed to shock troops at their private dwellings, and it was arranged that the double security doors to Hitler's chancellery were to be left unlocked at a given signal. That signal was to be the moment Hitler declared war on Czechoslovakia.

Hitler was expected to invade Czechoslovakia on October 1st, the day his ultimatum ended. All the preparations for the plot were already completed by September 15th, but England and France were procrastinating in giving the generals their assurances that they would come to their aid by declaring war on Germany the moment Hitler declared war on Czechoslovakia. The generals felt that their victory would be assured if they attacked Hitler's forces from within, while some of them were engaged fighting on the Western Front. They also felt that the German public would be on their side because it dreaded another war.

Though England and France gave their assurances on one of the last days (September 27th), a reflection on the causes of their delay may throw some light on the dynamics of Hitler's successes. The German generals repeatedly sent several prominent Germans to the Foreign Offices in London and Paris to ask for assurances. One German representative was asked by a British Foreign Service Officer if he did not think that their plot would be treasonous. When the French Chief-of-Staff, General Gamelin, discussed the assurances with the British Prime Minister Chamberlain, the latter was reluctant asking, "who can guarantee that Germany will not become Bolshevistic after the plot?" Conservative England preferred Hitler to the German Junkers. (Hoffmann, 1969).

It has already been pointed out that the German people voted for Hitler because they feared communism. It seems that the British people had the same motive when they allowed Hitler to rebuild the German Navy, to occupy the Saarland, and to annex the Sudetenland.

Since Hitler got what he wanted, the war on Czechoslovakia was never declared and the signal for the plot was never given. Had the plot taken place, Hitler would have been deposed and Europe's Jews would have been saved. It was not the anti-Semitism of the Germans which foiled the generals' plot, but the conservatism of the British who trusted Hitler more than the German nobility.

None of Hitler's victims received any significant aid from any organized forces. When 2000 communists were arrested after the Reichstags fire, Stalin made no efforts to rescue his Bolshevist comrades. Nobody came to the aid of the Social Democrats when they were arrested. When Hitler killed Roehm, a million of his own men did not fight Hitler as he had also killed their leaders. When Hitler wanted the Sudetenland, Chamberlain came to Munich and consented. When Hitler took Czechoslovakia, nobody came to its aid even though England and France had guaranteed its neutrality. When Hitler took Poland, England declared war on Germany, but was tactically unable to help. Worse yet, Russia came to Hitler's aid. Which group of Germans could have helped the Jews in the pre-war years? The German people could not have helped their own communist and socialist prisoners in the camps, therefore it is difficult to see how they could have helped the Jews in any organized way, as Goldhagen claims they could have had they not been anti-Semitic.

Chapter Fifteen

Entrapping the Jews

On a day when I suffered from hunger and cold more than I had ever suffered before, I was forced to write a postcard to my mother which read: "I am now in Camp Buchenwald where I am well treated and where I found interesting work. I am well and healthy and send you my best regards." I wrote this card on a day my group had carried bricks from dawn to dusk and had to stand outside in freezing weather for several hours. Just before we were allowed to lie down, we were ordered to march to a dimly lit hall where the contents of our message were dictated to us. Almost all of the Jews who were taken to concentration camps during the Crystal Night had to write similar misleading messages sometimes during the second week after their arrival. It was the beginning of the many lies and the false information which shrouded the entire annihilation process of the Jews.

Before the war, Hitler lied by playing down his intention to destroy the Jews in order to avoid diplomatic and economic sanctions. After the conquest of Poland, the lies continued so the Jews would not revolt or resist the deportation to the east. Even before Hitler came to power, he frequently mentioned to the foreign press that the Jews had nothing to fear. In 1930, for instance, in an interview with the *Times*, he declared that he and his party had nothing against decent Jews, but only against those who associated themselves with Bolshevism and must be regarded as enemies. To an American reporter, Hitler likewise emphasized that his party did not plan to deny rights to the Jews and that anti-Jewish phrases were only used to satisfy the public's expectations. (*Central Verein Zeitung*, 1930).

As already mentioned, when Hitler ordered the first boycott of the Jewish stores, he announced that he is merely defending himself against the anti-German propaganda in the foreign press. In the same vein, when Hitler decreed the Jews as "second class citizens", he declared that he does not do this to be unjust to the Jews, but rather to be fair to the Germans so that they will be economically equal to the Jews. He added, if this equality is reached then the Jews should be able to live in peace in Germany. Hitler, and his propaganda minister, Goebbels, made constant efforts to conceal their murderous anti-Semitic intentions from the outside world. During the 1936 Olympic year, all anti-Semitic propaganda was halted to impress the foreign visitors, by Germany's tranquility. Even Hitler's book, *Mein Kampf*, was greatly abridged and sanitized for its American publisher by the deletion of its most virulent anti-Semitic passages. When later U.S. Senator Alan Cranston, then a correspondent for the International News Service, returned from Germany after the Crystal Night, he was surprised to find this altered edition. To correct matters, he published his own unabridged version, which sold half a million copies, before he was sued for copyright infringement by the American publisher (Lipstadt, 1986).

Once the war had started, the Jews were deceived to believe that each step which brought them closer to their death was a step which would increase their chances of survival. More than any other man in the Nazi hierarchy, Reinhold Heydrich was responsible for programming the death of Jews, so that they would not resist and could not receive any organized help. Furthermore, Heydrich's scheme made it look to the outside world that the Jews were destroying themselves by their own administrative machinery.

Some months before the war started, Heydrich placed the "Association of German Jews" and its leader, the Chief Rabbi, Dr. Leo Baeck, under the jurisdiction of his own security police, the Gestapo. This new organization, named the "Jewish Self-Administration" (Selbstverwaltung) received all orders from Heydrich's office and had to relay them to the Jewish community through their bulletin, *The Jewish Courier*. Moreover, Dr. Baeck and his delegates became personally responsible for carrying out Heydrich's orders. In case of any noncompliance, the Jews themselves had to enforce Heydrich's orders through the Jewish Order Service (Ordnungsdienst)—a police unit wearing arm bands but no guns. The leaders of the Self-Administration had no bargaining power. They could not ask for more food or medical supplies, nor could they alter the number of Jews that they had to deliver to the armament factories or to the labor camps. In the final days of the expulsion from Berlin, it was the Jewish Order Service who had to execute Heydrich's order to select those Jews who were to stay in Germany for labor, and those who were lead to the railheads for transports to Poland.

Through the German, Czech, and Austrian Self-Administrations, the Nazis saved manpower and accomplished a practically riotless cleansing of the Berlin, Prague, and Viennese Jews. It has been claimed that it was easier for the Jews to bear their diminishing food rations, their living restrictions, and their final deportation orders because they were given by other Jews. However, the main reason for the frictionless deportation was the misinformation the Jews were given about the nature of their transports. For example, before their departure the Jews were usually given a packing list for items they were allowed to take along for their "resettlement" in Poland. This list included heavy work shoes, foods, and cooking utensils; items which made most of the deportees believe they were going to labor camps with cooking facilities.

In 1941 when the mass deportations of the Western Jews began, hardly a Jew or a non-Jew anticipated the extermination centers in Poland. It was not until May, 1941, that Heydrich forbade all Jews emigration "in view of the undoubtable imminent final solution of the Jewish question" (Days of Remembrance, 1991).

Up to this time, the Nazis supported the Jewish Emigration Agency which was still desperate for Jews to emigrate. The following letter is an example of such an attempt. It was written in 1940 by the Emigration Department of the Jewish Agency in Breslau to the author's mother who was a Jewish refugee in Havana, Cuba. The letter makes an urgent request for $400.00 which my mother's cousin and her one-year-old child needed to leave Germany for Shanghai. Since the emigration of the Jews had been sanctioned by the Nazis, most of the Jews believed that the transports to Poland were a "forced emigration."

(HILFSVEREIN)

Vom Herrn Reichsminister des Innern durch Verfügung von 31.10.1924 Nr. II 7781 als gemeinnützige Auswanderungsberatungsstelle für jüdische Auswanderer anerkannt

Beratungsstelle für Schlesien und angrenzende Teile der Lausitz

P/Wr.   Breslau, den   21. März 1940
               Wallstraße 9 / Telefon: 21357

Betrifft: _____
(Bei Beantwortung unbedingt anzugeben)

                         Frau
                         Irene Wolfsohn

                         Habana /Cuba

                         Calle 5a Nr. 89
                         entre 10 y 12

Betrifft Hedwig J a c o b Breslau Gabitzstr. 15
===

    Die Obengenannte muss mit ihrem im März vorigen Jahres geboren Kind zur Auswanderung gebracht werden.
Wir treten an Sie mit der Bitte heran, ihr ein Vorzeigegeld für Shanghai in Höhe von 400 $ zu besorgen.
Bitte geben Sie uns bald nach Erhalt des Briefes Antwort, was Sie in dieser Sache tun können, wobei wir Ihnen nochmals die Dringlichkeit des Falles vor Augen führen möchten.

                                    Hochachtungsvoll

The Nazis were concerned that the Jews would maintain their belief in "resettlement." As late as 1943, the Gestapo was still monitoring the opinions of the Jews in the deportation trains. For instance, when the first two deportation trains left Holland for the east, Otto Bene, Germany's Foreign Office representative in Holland, reported in May 1943 to the Foreign Office in Berlin, that the transports were proceeding without a "hitch", and that the legend is spreading among the Jews that the deportations from Holland are a true resettlement. And further, that there was an opinion in Jewish circles that the younger Jews were being sent first in order to begin building the resettlement camps, so the older ones could follow (Hilberg, 1985).

To show the world how humane the Nazis treated the Jews, Heydrich created Theresienstadt—his masterpiece of deception. In the Spring of 1942, he ordered all Czechs to move out of Theresianstadt, a small town in Czechoslovakia, where he established a special camp for Jewish ex-army officers, veterans, famous scientists, authors, and their relatives. Since these persons had friends and relatives in foreign countries, they were periodically ordered to write "I am well" notices. This was to show the world how civilized and humane the Nazis were, and that the reported concentration camp cruelties were inventions of disgruntled Jews and Bolshevists. Furthermore, Heydrich did not trust the anti-Semitism of the German army officers who he thought would object to any mistreatment of anyone who had once worn their uniform. Euphemistically, the internments in Thereisienstadt were called "change of residence." (Hilberg, 1985).

After the Nazis suffered reversals on all fronts, they no longer cared to keep up a good image, and the transports from Theresienstadt to Auschwitz began. Of a total of 140,000 Jews who had entered Theresienstadt, 30,000 had died and 88,000 were sent to Auschwitz and gassed in 1944. Four of Sigmund Freud's sisters who came to Theresienstadt from Vienna in 1941 were among them.

The deception of the Jews as to their final fate began with Heydrich's orders in 1938 and lasted until the very end of their annihilation. Even as late as August 1944, with the Red Army about to approach the Lodz Labor Camp, its 60,000 inmates were tricked into compliance. By that time, the Jews knew that any order to report to the railhead meant death in Auschwitz and therefore staged a sit-down strike in their workshops.

Not wanting to expend the necessary manpower to remove the Jews forcefully, the Ghetto Administrator, Hans Biebow, talked to them and assured them that they were going to a labor camp in Germany. He mentioned that their situation was different than it had been for other ghettos because the Soviets were approaching Lodz and all Germans in the city and in the work camps had to be evacuated. He assured them further that their work output had been very satisfactory and that their efforts were much needed in Germany. If they came to the train voluntarily they could take along forty pounds of baggage as well as their pots and pans, items which the bombing raids had made very scarce in Germany. The train trip, he mentioned, would take from 10 to 16 hours and food for this duration was already on the train. (A trip to Auschwitz, 120 miles away, would have taken five hours at the maximum). The Jews gave up their sit down strike and entered the trains which took them to Auschwitz where all 60,000 of them were gassed (Reitlinger, 1956).

Himmler, who after Heydrich's death, implemented the mass killings became obsessed with the secrecy of the entire destruction process. In literally thousands of directives which he and his SS leaders throughout Europe gave to arrest Jews and transport them to Auschwitz to be killed, the words killing, gassing, shooting, were never mentioned. Instead only the words "special treatment", the "solution", "final solution", or "East Solution" were allowed.

On almost every occasion when Himmler addressed his executioners, the commanders of his Mobile-Killing units, he stressed the secrecy of their mission. In Minsk, in 1941, he told them, "... we alone must carry this secret to our graves." And again in Posen in 1943, he reminded them that "...the disloyalty of any member, even if only in thought, must lead to his leaving the Order (the SS) and his life" (Broszat, 1968).

Himmler's warnings were not empty threats. There was an elaborate penal system set up for the insubordination of SS personnel which involved sentences in regular prisons, re-education, and concentration camps. In one case in 1942, for instance, the Nazi Medical Officer responsible for the health of Poles, received an order to resettle 200,000 Poles to avoid the spread of tuberculosis and to make room for German settlers. He was ordered to screen out old people, children, and those who had TB, a total of about 70,000 and treat them like Jews.

After receiving the order, the Medical Officer wrote a letter to Hitler several pages long, asking if this order was not a mistake. The letter was very deferential, containing many "my Fuhrer," and "only you can decide."

Nevertheless, doubt was expressed if it would not be better to let the children live, so that they might later serve Germany. And further: "...they are racially more closely related to us than the Jews, ...and many Poles would be willing to collaborate with us. One of their few good qualities is their love for their children, and if we kill them, their last spark of readiness to come to an accommodation will vanish" (Broszat, 1968, p. 380).

When Himmler came across this letter several months later, he ordered the writer to be consigned to a concentration camp for the duration of the war, because his views are dangerous to the state. This SS Medical Officer had used the word "kill" rather than "final solution."

Since the inception of the killing centers, Himmler was frantic about preserving their secrecy. He established them in Poland where he could clear large tracts of land and villages by sending the inhabitants to forced labor camps or to work on farms in Germany. In planning Auschwitz, Himmler cleared several villages of Poles to obtain a 17-square mile area for his prison compound. This large area allowed for a wide "no-man's land" security perimeter around each camp. Visitors could be shown one camp without being able to see what went on in a neighboring camp. Even high-ranking Nazi officials were not allowed to enter Auschwitz without Himmler's permission. When Hitler's Governor General, Hans Frank, attempted to visit some camps, he was turned down. Himmler discouraged him to visit Lublin and when he came to Auschwitz unannounced, his car was stopped at the gate and he was told that an epidemic had broken out in the camp. When Frank complained to Hitler, he was told that there might be executions in the camps but only of "insurgents" and that he should ask Himmler for detailed information (Laquer, 1980).

There was even much secrecy about various activities within a camp, especially about the various medical experiments which were conducted without the inmates' consent and at times without their knowledge. When Himmler intended to ship male and female Jews back to Germany for work in the war production plants, he wanted to make sure that they would never be able to propagate. In cooperation with several physicians, he conducted a secret sterilization experiment. The Jews in question received repeated doses of radiation aimed at their lower abdomens. They were called to a counter and asked to fill out certain forms while they were radiated—never knowing that they received repeated doses of radiation.

The new arrivals in Auschwitz were mislead up to the last minute. When the killing centers were overcrowded they were held in "special quarters" awaiting to be gassed. One set of gas chambers had the inscriptions "Wash and Disinfection Hall." The victims had to undress there and while stepping naked into the chamber they were given a receipt for their clothing.

Chapter Sixteen

Reprisals

Goldhagen asserts that it was the anti-Semitism of the Germans which made them passive bystanders to the destruction of the Jews. He supports this assertion by the fact that the Germans did not help the Jews in any institutionalized way. In this chapter, however, it will be shown that any resistance to the Nazis brought swift reprisals and that it was the devastating effect of these reprisals, and not necessarily the anti-Semitism of the Germans, which deterred any inside or outside group from helping the Jews in an organized way.

Hitler had two distinct ways of killing his victims, a secret and a public one. Millions of people were arrested through secret orders, shipped to fictitious destinations, and killed in off-limit areas. In contrast, a certain number of executions were officially announced and carried out in full view of the public to warn all those who might disobey Hitler's orders. As already mentioned, one of these highly publicized reprisals was the event of the Crystal Night. One German diplomat was shot in Paris and the next day, 30,000 German Jews were on their way to concentration camps. It was the largest, swiftest, and perhaps the most successful reprisal action known in recent times. Like Hitler's previous coups, it was tactically well prepared, kept top secret, catching the victims defenseless and in total surprise.

Hitler's reprisal action, the Crystal Night, was staged six years after he came to power, after he had thoroughly destroyed his opposing forces inside Germany, and after the outside forces (England, France, and Poland), had agreed that he occupy part of Czechoslovakia. Hence, while I was on the train transport from Breslau to Buchenwald I did not expect anyone to rescue me. Even in retrospect, I cannot imagine who could have saved us. Perhaps we could have saved ourselves by killing the guard in our train compartment. We were 20 Jews, not handcuffed, and the guard was sitting on a single seat with his pistol in his holster. Any two or three of us could have overpowered him. But during the actual trip I dismissed this thought immediately. I did not know the other Jews sitting close to me. We were not allowed to talk or touch the drawn window shades. Most of us did not have anything to drink for the last 24 hours, and we did not know where we were, nor where we were going. We were in a physiological and psychological no-man's land. We obeyed all orders because most of us believed that we would come back alive, though only half of us did.

Hitler did not have to fight any battles to conquer almost all of Europe. Without any warning, his planes bombarded Rotterdam on May 10th, 1940, destroying most of the city within a few hours. Fearing that more cities would be bombed, the Dutch Queen fled Holland and the Germans moved in without any resistance. A similar situation happened in Belgium a few days later, when the Germans began marching through Belgium to circumvent the Maginot Line in order to occupy France. King Leopold tried to block the Germans from moving through Liege, but the Germans threatened to level the city. In order to prevent this destruction, the Belgian Army offered no resistance. The unopposed move through Belgium made it possible for the German Army to occupy France without fighting. This speedy conquest frightened Stalin, who did everything to appease Hitler. Russia began supplying Germany with trainloads of grain, oil, and other important minerals. Furthermore, Stalin refrained from carrying out maneuvers and did not put his defense forces on full alert, though he had good evidence that the Germans were mobilizing to attack Russia. Stalin's military neglect, and his economic support allowed the Germans to capture 12,000 Russian tanks, 9,000 aircraft, and 800,000 Russian soldiers in the first five weeks of the war without hardly losing any of their men or equipment (Day of Remembrance, 1991).

Through the fear of reprisals, having their cities bombed, Hitler had conquered almost all of Europe and a good part of Russia. He had become the absolute ruler of about 300 million people living in 19 different countries. Through the most devastating reprisals, he forced the populations of these countries to obey his occupation rules, to round up Jews, to supply goods, and to send laborers to Germany. Early in 1940, for example, Dutch and German SS men began destroying the synagogues in Amsterdam. Trying to prevent this destruction, Dutch Gentiles and Jews fought the SS, whereby one SS man was killed. As a reprisal, the Germans killed six Jews and sent 400 of them to concentration camps in Germany. When this reprisal action was publicly announced by the German occupation authorities, almost 20,000 Dutch workers staged a sympathy strike, bringing transportation and war production to a standstill in several Dutch cities. In response to this strike, General Christiansen, the commander of the German Occupation Army, ordered an even tougher reprisal—the death penalty for every striker who did not return within three days. In addition, fines were leveled for each Dutch citizen who earned over 10,000 gulden per year (Hilberg, 1985).

As Hitler's puppet governments became more firmly established, their reprisal tactics became even more massive. In December 1941, when one German officer was slightly wounded in Paris, 100 Jews were shot immediately and 1,000 Eastern Jews living in Paris were deported to camps in Poland. Additionally, the Jewish Counsel of Paris was ordered to collect one billion Francs from the Paris Jews for retribution payment to the German occupation authority.

As described by MacDonald (1989), perhaps the most cruel and widespread reprisal was carried out against the Czechs to revenge Heydrich's death and to find his attackers. Reinhard Heydrich was almost solely responsible for the creation and the training of the light motorized killing troops (Einsatzkommandos) who machine-gunned close to a million Jews on the outskirts of Polish and Russian cities. Though Heydrich was Chief of the German Gestapo, he shared Germany's top destruction command with

Heinrich Himmler, leader of the German SS. By provoking unrest in Czechoslovakia, Heydrich convinced Hitler to appoint him governor of the Czech Protectorate where he was the sole ruler, where no one would interfere with his despotism. As the "protector" of the Czechs, he sent thousands of Jews to Polish camps and thousands of Czechs to labor camps in Germany. He was particularly vicious to the Czechs who had served in the army.

The Czech Army in exile planned to kill Heydrich through special parachute agents trained in England. Dropped into the Czech mountains in December 1941, they were finally able to carry out their attack on May 27, 1942. Two parachutists, Gabcik and Kubis waylaid Heydrich in his open Mercedes. Gabcik's sten gun failed, but Kubis' bomb injured Heydrich who fainted after a few moments. Both Gabcik and Kubis escaped from the attack scene and the most extensive man hunt and the most severe reprisals followed.

The entire village of Lidice was to be destroyed as it was suspected that some of its inhabitants had harbored the parachutists. In the evening at 9:30 P.M. the village was cordoned off. All males over fifteen, 199 of them, were shot. The women and children were shipped to camps in Germany, except 9 children who were sent to German families for Aryanization. Jews from the nearby concentration camp Terezin were called in to bury the dead. Every house in Lidice was leveled to the ground. As no evidence was found in Lidice, the search continued and several other villages met the same fate as Lidice. In Prague, approximately 21,000 Czech police and Waffen SS searched 36,000 houses not finding any clues. Through Himmler, Hitler gave the order to execute 30,000 Czechs, but they also promised immunity to all those who would write a letter to the Gestapo condemning the assassination and providing information. The Gestapo received 2,000 letters within three days . One of the parachutists gave his comrades away. His letter read: "Cease searching for the assassins ...cease arresting and executing innocent people. I can't stand it any more...."

The parachutists, a group of seven, were hiding in the crypt of the Karel Boromejski Church. When they were found, they were flushed out with flame throwers and poison gas. They fought back until they ran out of ammunition, killing themselves with their last bullets. Gruesome interrogations began for their relatives and for the members of the "safe houses" which had harbored them. The heads of all seven parachutists were impaled on spikes at the interrogation center. They tried to get confessions from people by making them drunk or by beating them. To one person, they showed the severed head of his mother. Within three months after Heydrich's assassination, more than 3,000 Czechs were arrested of whom 1,357 were executed. In addition, 3,000 Jews from Prague were sent to death camps in Poland in special trains marked "for Heydrich's assassination." A total of 252 relatives and helpers of the parachutists were condemned to death and executed in Prague on Sept. 29th. The bishop and the clergy connected with the hiding place, the Karel Boromejski Church, were executed and the Orthodox Church was dissolved and their property confiscated throughout Czechoslovakia. The reprisals continued. About 4,000 relatives of Czech exiles, including the relatives of the former Czech president Eduart Benes, were rounded up and sent to an interment camp in Moravia as hostages.

The Nazis had millions of Jews in ghettos, millions of Russians and Poles in prison and labor camps while they were fighting in Russia and in Africa, in addition to occupation forces in about a dozen European countries. Hence, it is reasonable to assume, as Goldhagen does, that every German must have had a hand in persecuting Jews and other victims. But in reality, the Nazis were delegating most of their "dirty" work to their victims, actually to their prospective victims. For example, when Goebbels ordered all Jews to be cleared out of Berlin during the summer of 1942, train transports for 1,000 Jews had to be readied on certain days. For this purpose the Jewish leadership of the Jewish Self-Administration had to prepare maps for the Gestapo encircling the houses where Jews lived. A Jewish Order Service was created to accompany the Gestapo to the apartments of the

Jews to help them pack and to lead them to collecting places (emptied apartments) where they were guarded for a day or two until their departure by train.

The members of the Jewish Order Service wore a red armband. They were also called "Jew Police" (Judenpolizei), "Fetching Service", or "Roundup Commando". Before they were selected for their task, they were warned by their Jewish leader that they would be shot and their relatives would be sent east if they refused their duty, if they told anyone when the transports were leaving, or if they let anyone escape. In the entire destruction process of the European Jews, the Nazis did very little work. From the top echelon down to the local Gestapo agents they just issued decrees upon decrees, gave orders, and shot those who did not obey them. They also shot others who did obey their orders to teach the population a lesson.

With secret as well as public executions, the Nazis subjected millions of Czech, Dutch, French, and Poles to follow their orders. With a minimum of manpower, they prevented all uprisings. In France, for instance, they ruled many middle-sized towns by placing just one Gestapo agent in each of the offices of the mayor, the postmaster, the police, and the station master. If these agents had any suspicion of non-cooperation or resistance, they would order Hitler's "Night and Fog" arrest for the person in question. In order to keep the French population calm, Hitler wanted their underground resistance fighters to be arrested in secret, without witnesses.

On the other hand, anyone who disobeyed the occupation authorities openly, who wounded a German soldier, who hid a Jew, listened to British broadcasts, etc., was publicly punished. Motorized or parachute SS units (Feldjaeger) would arrive within hours where an incident took place. If they could not find the accused, they were likely to take a number of hostages from nearby tenement houses and imprison them. If any weapons were found or if there was evidence of any plot, the accused were summarily executed. In many French towns in their market squares and in remote court yards are memory plaques honoring the victims murdered by these SS commandos.

The only armed resistance which inflicted some minor losses on the SS was staged by the Jews in the Warsaw ghetto in April 1943. The Warsaw ghetto consisted of about 80 city blocks holding about 380,000 Jews. The entire ghetto was fenced in, with machine guns and artillery in strategic places. There were certain guarded gates through which those Jews who worked in factories outside the ghetto could leave and enter. Most Jews, however, worked in factories inside the ghetto manufacturing uniforms and shoes for the SS and the German Army. In July 1942, the Jewish Council, through which the Nazis administered the ghetto, received the order to ready 60,000 "nonproductive elements" for "resettlement" (Aussiedlung). Ten thousand Jews per day were to report at the ghetto's railhead each morning for transport to Treblinka. Since it was already rumored that the Jews going there might be put into forced labor camps or perhaps be killed, there were no volunteers for the transports. Hence, each Jewish Order policeman was ordered to bring seven "unproductive" Jews to the railhead on the mornings the trains were to leave. If he arrived with less than seven, he himself was grabbed by the SS and loaded onto the train.

Turmoil and despair arose in the ghetto. The head of the Jewish Council, Adam Czerniakow, committed suicide. His successors argued that the 60,000 persons must be delivered in order to save the remaining 320,000. Several younger Jews, who had previously been active in the Polish Communist and Zionist Parties, considered the Jewish Council a mere relay mechanism for implementing SS orders. They made plans for an armed resistance secretly organizing into fighting units and securing arms through the Polish underground. It took months to obtain and hide 2 machine guns, 20 rifles (the entire supply of the Polish underground), several hundred pistols, hand grenades, and explosives. They also began to construct individual dugouts which connected to the Warsaw sewer system under the ruse of building air raid shelters. The young resistance organizers shot the Jewish chief of the Order Police and his second in command thus gaining internal control of the ghetto (Reitlinger, 1956).

In the meantime, the trains from the ghetto's railhead kept leaving almost every morning, each carrying up to 5,000 Jews to Treblinka. Within several months, 300,000 Jews had been deported from the ghetto. Only 70,000 Jews, all workers in the ghetto industries, were left by January 1943. But when Himmler visited Warsaw during this month, he still wanted 8,000 more Jews to be removed. This time the German SS, with the help of Hungarian and Baltic SS units, entered the ghetto unannounced and were able to lead 6,500 working Jews away. There was individual resistance whereby a German police captain was severely wounded. Subsequent to this incident, Himmler ordered the entire ghetto to be cleared and razed to the ground. He ordered his SS units to plan an attack and secured some backup help from the regular German army. After thoroughly surrounding the ghetto at 3 A.M. on the morning of April 19, 1943, the first Nazi tank entered. It was blown up and the SS was met with fire. They withdrew with casualties. They returned and withdrew again in a seesaw battle which lasted for days. Each time, the Nazis returned with new weapons (mortars and flame throwers) and reinforcements. They began flooding the sewers and throwing explosives into them, which the Jews were using as fox holes. They used flame throwers to set the houses on fire . The Jews suffered tremendous losses but held out heroically for three weeks. On May 8th, their commander, Mordechai Anielewicz, was killed and a week later, Warsaw's SS commander, Jurgen Stroop, blew up the great Tlomacki Synagogue in the center of the city to "celebrate" his victory over the ghetto. When the battle was over, several thousand Jews were dead in the ghetto's debris above and in the flooded sewers below. A total of 56,000 were captured. Of those, 7,000 were shot, 21,000 sent to killing centers, and 28,000 to labor camps. In contrast, the German casualties consisted of 16 dead and 86 wounded.

The ghetto riots and other uprisings in Holland, France and Czechoslovakia did not relieve the sufferings of Hitler's victims. To the contrary, they shortened the lives of the rioters and of thousands of others who were killed in reprisal actions. To a certain extent, they even played into the Nazis' hands as it gave them an excuse for further brutal murders. Though the uprisings did not save any lives, they were morally uplifting to the heroes who preferred fighting to month-long starvation and beatings while awaiting their death.

Chapter Seventeen

Hitler's Irrationality

To the world, but particularly to the European statesmen and to the German Jews, Hitler often appeared to be irrational. He killed Roehm and hundreds of his Brown Shirt leaders because they wanted war, while he dismissed some of his generals because they wanted peace. He signed a ten year non-aggression pact with Poland in 1934 with a country he wanted to destroy—what he actually did five years later. Hitler mentioned in his early speeches in Munich that the Jews should have been gassed in the First World War, but after he became chancellor ten years later, he announced repeatedly that the German Jews had nothing to fear. After having called the Russian Bolshevists "hordes of brutal murderers" for 20 years, he signed a secret friendship pact with Stalin.

Among his many contradictory orders, he sent some Jews who worked in the defense industries in Germany to Auschwitz, an act which Goldhagen considers irrational and self-destructive and indicative of a deep-seated, unconscious anti-Semitism. In this chapter it will be shown that Hitler's contradictory rhetoric and his apparent irrationality were part of his rationally pursued master plan—to kill the Jews and enslave the Russians. Moreover, it will be shown that much of his success was due to this apparent irrationality. Hitler often changed, and at times even contradicted, the objectives of his master plan, whenever it was to his advantage. He did this cunningly to catch his victims off guard, and also to please foreign diplomats from whom he wanted certain concessions.

With respect to the Jews, Hitler's apparent irrationality was most damaging. His hours-long illogical speeches in the early Munich days made us, and most of his other enemies, believe that he was an irrational crank who could never be a successful politician. Hence, when Hitler suddenly declared martial law in February 1933, we Jews had no plan for any defense, and no plans for an alliance with the communists or socialists—Hitler's other opponents who were also persecuted. There was no escape route and from that day on, we could only play a submissive role not knowing which additional restriction the next day would bring. Our restrictions increased gradually, but there were also periods of easements which most of us took mistakenly as signs of hope.

During the 1936 Olympic year, there was hope when some anti-Semitic posters disappeared from public display cases, and also, when Goering approved the establishment of the Jewish Cultural Association (Kulturbund). This allowed the Jews to produce and direct their own plays and musical performances, though it was forbidden to perform "typical" German authors and composers, such as Schiller, Goethe, Wagner, Strauss, and others. About half of all German Jews became members of the Kulturbund (Friedlaender, 1997). Its frequent performances provided the Jewish community with a pleasant cultural coherence in its otherwise restricted life.

Few of us realized that the formation of the Kulturbund had other purposes than comforting the Jews. It helped the Gestapo to establish a Jewish Index (Judenkartei), an attempt to obtain a dossier on every German and on some influential foreign Jews. Additional data was obtained from membership lists of Gestapo-approved Jewish sports clubs, language schools, etc. Furthermore, the Kulturbund was an early model of the Jewish Self-Administration instituted by Heydrich at the beginning of the war and also for the Jewish Ghetto Counsels (Judenrat) in Poland. It gave the appearance of self-rule though the parameters were strictly prescribed by the Gestapo.

The Kulturbund had still another purpose. In the eyes of the Germans and foreign diplomats, it made the Nazis appear very civil. Most of us Jews looked healthy and were well dressed when attending our cultural evenings so that it appeared to the public that we were still well treated and that there was no urgent need to help us.

Though we did not realize it at the time, any abating of Hitler's anti-Semitism was merely for diplomatic purposes and stalling for time. After the British Prime minister, Neville Chamberlain, and the French Premier Eduard Daladier had signed the Peace Treaty in Munich, Hitler no longer needed his facade of civility. Hence, only six weeks after the German troops had moved into the Sudetenland, the Propaganda Minister, Goebbels, staged the Crystal Night. Though he did this without Hitler's permission, Hitler condoned it after it had happened. When Himmler and Goering suggested that Goebbels be relieved of his office, Hitler replied that one propaganda chief was more valuable to him than several generals.

The Crystal Night told us that our existence in Germany was coming to an end, but again we had no idea what that end would be. The Nazis wanted us to emigrate, but they had taken most of our money and only few of us who had relatives or friends abroad, were able to obtain visas and tickets. Our money was taken in the form of a "fleeing tax" and an "atonement tax". The latter was an assessment of one billion marks for the death of the German consular officer in Paris and for the damage for the broken showcase windows which the Nazis smashed on Goebbels command. As late as January 1939, Goering urged his subordinates to set up offices throughout Germany to speed up the emigration of Jews. He also asked to further the Rublee plan, a negotiation between an American business man and the former German finance minister, Hjalmer Schacht, which was taking place in London. This plan proposed that the German government pays for the Jew's visa expense and that the Jew or a guarantor would buy a certain amount of German goods after his or her emigration. This "rescue attempt" was to save several hundred thousand Jews, but it did not materialize.

Shortly after Goering issued his appeal for emigration, Hitler suggested for the first time that the Jews might serve as hostages and stay in Germany. He announced on January 30, 1939 that the European Jews would be destroyed if the world Jewry would start another World War, though it was Hitler who started this war just seven months later by invading Poland.

Soon after the war started, all emigration was halted and all Jews were assigned to labor commandos or defense work. The hostage idea was brought up again in 1940 when Hitler, on Heydrich's suggestion, envisioned all Jews to be shipped to Madagascar. Hitler wanted all Jews to be in one place, so that it would be easier to inflict reprisals on them in case the American Jews would attack Germany. Some Jews from southern Germany were already on their way to Marseilles for embarkment when the Madagascar Project was halted because the British Mediterranean Fleet had not surrendered as the Nazis had hoped.

By December 1941, Hitler had occupied 19 European countries and an area of Russia which reached from Leningrad in the north to Odessa in the south and to the outskirts of Moscow on the east. Hitler had control over 300 million people, inclusive of five million Jews and three-and-a-half million Russian war prisoners. He had obtained all this by lies and treaties, by bombing Rotterdam, and by threats and reprisals—without fighting a single major battle. In spite of some apparent detours and contradictions, in the main, he had rationally followed his master plan.

During the first nine years of his dictatorship, he had made no irrational decisions counter to his very existence—decisions which Goldhagen considers manifestation of a deep-seated unconscious anti-Semitism. Hitler's bad decisions came later in 1942 and 1943, when his troops experienced their first reversals. He refused to rescind the order to kill Russian prisoners when his generals reported that this practice had stiffened the Russian resistance and hindered the German advances.

Hitler forbade his troops to retreat. This often caused great and unnecessary hardships on them. When this was pointed out to Hitler, he replied to his commanders that they should not avoid being harsh on their men, and that it did not bother

Frederick the Great when he lost soldiers. Hitler's most irrational decision, and perhaps his most fateful one, was his order to General Paulus not to move to the rear in an attempt to break out of his Russian encirclement. Paulus felt that he could break out by using a pincer movement on the Russian forces with the help of General Manstein attacking simultaneously from the rear. But Hitler, angered by some of the losses which he thought his generals caused, forbade Paulus to move backwards, and did now allow him to surrender. He appointed General Paulus as field marshal to encourage him to obey his orders and "to fight to his last man and to his last cartridge." Paulus surrendered three days later on Feb. 02, 1943. Ninety-one thousand men were taken prisoner by the Russians. The entire 6th army was destroyed. It was the turning point of Hitler's war (Fest, 1974).

On the home front, Hitler made likewise counterproductive decisions. Goebbels, the Propaganda Minister wanted to make Germany free of Jews and ordered more and more Jews to be shipped to Poland, while Albert Speer, the War Production Minister, wanted the skilled Jews, mainly the lens grinders, to remain in war production in Germany. Hitler decided in Goebbels' favor. The mass killings of Russian and Jewish prisoners of war who were imprisoned in concentration camps inside Germany, were shot at a rate of about 1,000 per day, while labor was badly needed for underground installations.

It is difficult to ascribe Hitler's irrational decisions to an unconscious anti-Semitism as Goldhagen does. On the winning side, Hitler's decisions were much more rational than they were on the losing side. Hitler would scream at generals refusing to take his suggestions. His irrationality seemed to have been fed by an intense hatred; not only by a hatred of Jews but also by a hatred for Russians, the Polish nobility and the German general class. After the plot on his life, he ordered the first batch of eight generals to be killed by slow hanging. The rope noose was to be fixed in such a way that it would not break their necks but would choke them slowly. During this process he ordered their pants to be pulled down so that they would be left hanging naked. Hitler had the entire hanging filmed and viewed it in the evening of the day the hanging took place. Studying Hitler's cruelty, it is difficult to discern where his anti-Semitism ends and where his brutality begins. Hitler was not only an anti-Semitic beast but he was also monstrously antihuman.

References and Bibliography

Adler, H.G. (1969). *The Jews in Germany: From the Enlightenment to National Socialism*. Notre Dame, Ind: University of Notre Dame Press.

Barkai, A. (1989). *From Boycott to Annihilation: The Economic Struggle of German Jews, 1933-1943*. Hanover, N. H.: University Press of New England (published for Brandeis University Press).

Bain, A. (1940). *Theodore Herzl: A Biography*. Philadelphia: The Jewish Publication Society of America.

Baynes, N.H. (1942). *The Speeches of Adolf Hitler: April 1922 – August 1939* London: Oxford University Press.

Bieber, H. (1970). *Anti-Semitism as A Reflection of Social Economic and Political Tensions in Germany 1880-1933*. In: D. Bronsen (Ed) *Jews and Germans from 1860 to 1933*. (pp.33-77). Heidelberg: Carl Winter Universitatsverlag.

Black, E. (1984). *The Transfer Agreement: The Untold Story of the Secret Agreement between the Third Reich and Jewish Palestine* New York: Macmillan; London: Collier Macmillan.

Braunbuch über Reichstagsbrand und Hitler-Terror I [Hauptbd.]. (1933) Basel: Universum Bücherei.

Broszat, M. (1965). *Anatomie des SS-Staates*. Bd. II, Freiburg. i.B.: Walter-Verlag.

Chamberlain, H.S. (1906). *Die Grundlagen des neunzehnten. Jahrhunderts*. 6th Ed. Munich: Bruckmann.

Central Verein Zeitung (1930). Oct. 24th.

Dawidowicz, L. (1975). *The War Against The Jews*. New York: Holt Rinehart & Winston.

Days of Remembrance (1991). United States Holocaust Memorial Counsel.

Deutsche, W. (1885). In: R.A. Kann, *German Speaking Jewry During Austria-Hungary's Constitutional Era (1867-1918). Jewish Social Studies*, 10 (July 1948). pp. 245-249.

Ettinger, S. (1978). *The Jews in Russia at The Outbreak of the Revolution*. In Ed. L. Kochan, *The Jews in Soviet Russia since 1917*. pp.15-29. London: Oxford University Press.

Fest, J. (1974) *Hitler*. N.Y.: Harcourt Brace Jovanovich.

Freeden, H. (1964). *Judisches Theater in Nazi Deutschland*. Tübingen: Mohr.

Gay, R. (1992). *The Jews of Germany: An Historical Portrait*. New Haven: Yale University Press.

Gilman, S. (1979). *The Rediscovery of the Eastern Jews: German Jews in the East, 1980-1918*. In: D. Bronsen, *Jews and Germans from 1860-1933: The Problematic Symbiosis*. Heidelberg: Carl Winter. Universitatsverlag.

Gobineau, J. (1859). *The Inequality of The Races*. Paris.

Goldhagen, D.J. (1996). *Hitler's Willing Executioners: Ordinary Germans and the Holocaust*. New York: A. Knopf. : distributed by Random House.

Hackett, D.A. (1995). *The Buchenwald Report*. Boulder, CO: Westview Press.

Heins, H. (1980). *Adolf Hitler: Monolge im Fuhrer Hauptquartier 1941-1944* Hamburg: Albert Kraus Verlag.

Hilberg, R. (1961). *The Destruction of The European Jews*. Chicago: Quadrangle Books.

Hilberg, R. (1985). *The Destruction of The European Jews*. New York: Holmes & Meier.

Hilderbrand, K. (1984). *The Third Reich*. London: George Allen & Unwin.

Hitler, A. (1943). *Mein Kampf*. Boston: Sentry Paperback.

Hoffmann, P. (1969). *Widerstand, Staatsstreich, Attentat; der Kampf der Opposition. gegen Hitler*. Munich: R. Piper.

Höss, R. (1958). *Kommandant in Auschwitz;autobiographische Aufzeichnungen*. Stuttgart: Deutsche Verlags-Anstalt.

Kaznelson, S. (1962). (Ed.) *Juden im deutschen Kulturbereich*. Berlin: Judischer Verlag.

Kracauer, I. (1925) *Geschichte der Juden in Frankfurt am Main*. Frankfurt A.M.: In Kommission bei Kauffmann.

Krausnick, H. (1965). *Anatomie des SS-Staates: Judenverfolgung*. Freiburg i.B.: Walter-Verlag.

Krueger, K. (1943). *I Was Hitler's Doctor*. New York: Biltmore Publishing Company.

Langmuir, G.I. (1990). *Toward A Definition of Anti-Semitism*. Berkeley: University of California Press.

Laqueur, W. (1980). *The Terrible Secret: The Suppression of Information About Hitler's "Final Solution"*. Boston: Little Brown.

Lipstadt, D. (1986). *Beyond Belief: The American Press and the Coming of the Holocaust, 1933-1945*. New York: The Free Press; London: Collier Macmillan.

Long, W. (1968). *The New Nazis of Germany*. Philadelphia: Chilton Book Company.

Luther, M. (1523), (1543). *That Jesus Was A Born Jew*. Vol. 11, 1523. *Of Jews and Their Lies*, 1543, Vol. 50, p. 336 in Complete works, Weimar Edition. Also discussed in **H. Bornkamm**. *Luther's World of Thought*. St. Louis: Concordia Publishing House, 1958, pp. 226-233.

MacDonald, C. A. (1989). *The Killing of SS Obergruppenfuhrer Reinhard Heydrich*. New York: The Free Press.

McKale, D. (1977). *The Swastika Outside Germany*.
Kent, Ohio: Kent State University Press.

New York Times. Front Page Reports from June 2-June 8, 1939.

Niewyk, D. (1980). *The Jews in Weimar Germany*.
Baton Rouge: Louisiana State University Press.

Pulzer, P. (1964). *The Rise of Political Anti-Semitism in Germany and Austria*.
New York: Wiley.

Ragins, S. (1980). *Jewish Responses to Anti-Semitism in Germany 1870-1914*.
Cincinnati: Hebrew Union College Press.

Reitlinger, G. (1956). *Die Endlösung: Hitler's Versuch der Ausrottung der Juden Europas, 1939-1945* (The Final Solution).
Berlin: Colloquium Verlag Berlin.

Remak, J. (1969). *The Nazi Years: A Documentary History*.
Englewood Cliffs, N.J.: Prentice-Hall.

Ribbentrop, J. von. (1938). see: Hilberg, R. *Destruction of the European Jews*.
Vol II, p. 395.

Rinott, M. (1976). *The Zionist Organization and The Hilfsverein : Cooperation and Conflict 1901-1914*. In: Leo Baeck Institute Yearbook. vol. 21, no. 1 pp. 261-278.

Schapiro, L. (1978). *Introduction*, In: L. Kochan *The Jews in Soviet Russia Since 1917*. pp. 1-14. London: Oxford University Press.

Schechtman, J. (1978). *The U.S.S.R., Zionism, and Israel*. In: Ed. L. Kochan, *The Jews in Soviet Russia Since 1917*. pp. 106-131. London: Oxford University Press.

Scheffler, W. (1964). *Der Nationalsozialismus*. In: H.H. Hartwich (Ed.) *Politik im 20 Jahrhundert*. Braunschweig: Georg Westermann Verlag.

Scholom, G. (1979). *On The Social Psychology of The Jews in Germany: 1900-1933*. In: D. Bronsen (Ed.) *Jews and Germans from 1860 to 1933: The Problematic Symbiosis*. pp. 9-32. Heidelberg: Carl Winter Universitatsverlag.

Schwarzschild, S. (1979). *Germans and Judaism*. Herman Cohen's *Normative Paradigm of the German-Jewish Symbiosis*. In: D. Bronsen (Ed.) *Jews and Germans from 1860 to 1933*. pp. 129-172. Heidelberg: Carl Winter Universitatsverlag.

Second Brownbook. (1934) London

Sterling, E. (1969) *Judenhass: die Anfange des Politischen Anti-Semitismus in Deutschland (1815-1850)*. Frankfurt am Main: Europaische Verlags-Anstalt

Wiedemann, F. (1937). In: **H. Krausnick**. (1965) *Anatomie des SS-Staates*. p. 325. Freiburg i.B.: Walter-Verlag

About the Author

The author, Frank Wesley is a professor emeritus at Portland State University where he taught for over fifty years. He has written books and papers in child development, sex-role behavior, his personal recollections of the field of psychology, and the history of the Holocaust. He holds a BA degree from Reed College; MS and Ph. D. degrees from Washington State University; and a Ph. D. *rare naturum* degree from Hanover, Germany. He has held professional appointments in Germany, France, and Russia. In 1990, he was named a fellow of the American Psychological Association.

Appendix

The following pages to this revised edition contain a selection of documents, artifacts and photographs that not only briefly represent the author's life, but also illuminate the concepts set forth in this book that anti-Semitism was not genetically inherent within Germany and its people.

Familienstammbuch

This remarkable document dating from 1895 in Breslau is the official family record of Jakob and Irene Wolfsohn's immediate family from their marriage in 1911, through the births (and one death) of their children. The author can be found in the fourth listing under the second section entitled children (II. Kinder) as Franz Helmut Wolfsohn.

The Familienstammbuch as a government record is inclusory, if not demographic, evidence of the German citizenship and nationality of those recorded. One's religion only seems necessary as a matter of matrimonial record. With inclusive dates from 1881 through 1922, there is no historical semblance during this time period of subordinate treatment of German-Jews.

This reproduction continues over the next 4 pages.

Dieses Familien-Stammbuch ist bei jeder Meldung dem Standesbeamten vorzulegen.

Familienstammbuch

des

Reichsbund
Jakob Wolfsohn
in Breslau

Ministerial-Erlaß v. 29. April 1895.

Minist. Blatt f. die gesammte innere Verw. pro 1895, Seite 135.

1. Die Standesbeamten werden hiermit ausdrücklich ermächtigt, auf Ersuchen der Betheiligten in den ihnen von diesen vorgelegten Büchern die Jahreszahl in Betracht kommenden Geburten, Heirathen und Sterbefälle zu vermerken, auf Grund der in den Standesregistern stattgehabten Eintragungen zu vermerken und deren Eintragungen in deren Büchern mit ihrer amtlichen Unterschrift und ihrem Dienstsiegel zu versehen.

2. Den Standesbeamten wird hiermit ausdrücklich untersagt, für ihre Mitwirkung bei der Ausstellung der Bücher irgend eine Vergütung für sich oder ihr Büreaupersonal zu verlangen oder anzunehmen.

Berlin, den 29. April 1895.

Der Minister des Innern.
von Köller.

Bestellungen an Verlag Oberschlesischer Dorfkalender in Beuthen.

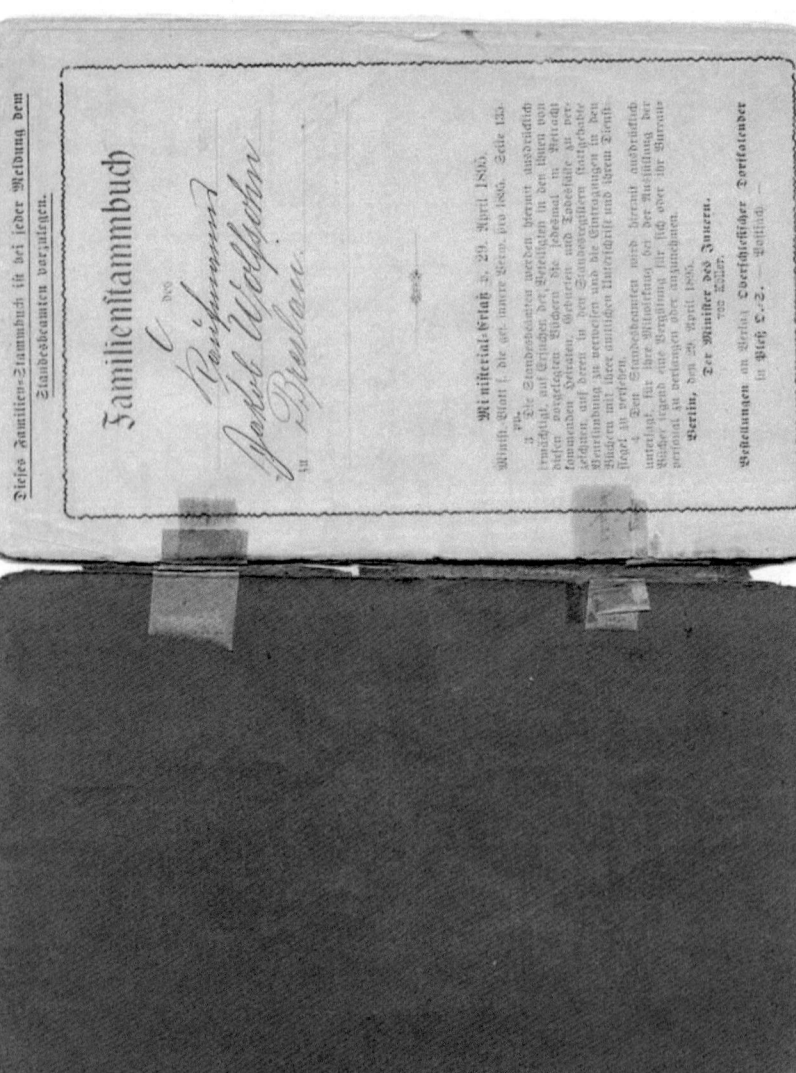

Namen und Stand der Ehegatten	Religion	Geburtstag und Geburtsort	Namen, Stand und Wohnort deren Eltern	Zeit und Ort der Eheschließung und Nr. des Registers	Beglaubigung des Standesbeamten mit Unterschrift u. Siegel	Zeit u. Ort des Todes u. Nr. des Sterberegisters	Beglaubigung des Standesbeamten mit Unterschrift u. Siegel
I. Ehegatten							
Bertel Wolfschcin Kaufmann	mos.	18 August 1881 Neustadt Kreis Neustadt Oberschlesien	N.N. Wolfschcin Kaufmann jetzt wohnhaft in Neustadt, Bahnstr. 21. Lisbeth geborene Heclick, wohnh. Neustadt/Oberschles.	22 Mai 1911 Breslau Nr. 287. Band IV 259. II.	[signature + seal]		
Franz Luise geb. Jacob	mos.	29 Januar 1892 Lissa i./P. Kreis Fraustadt	Aron Jacob Kaufmann Wohnort geboren von Lissa, jetzt wohnhaft Breslau				

II. Kinder

A Geburten

Lfd. Nr.	Vor- und Zunamen	Zeit u. Ort der Geburt	Standesamt und Nr. des Geburtsregisters	Unterschrift
1	Martin Wolfsohn	17. Juli 1906 Breslau II N°1548/12.7		Wichorzyk
2	Margaret Maria Wolfsohn	17. Mai 1909 Breslau II 1139/13		Wichorzyk
3	Thora Benjamin Agnes Wolfsohn	Breslau II 25.9.15 N°4424/15		389 formulas Wichorzyk
4	Franz Siegmund Wolfsohn	11. ... 1912 Breslau		Josef Fürther

B Todesfälle

Zeit und Ort des Todes	Standesamt und Nr. des Sterberegisters	Beglaubigung des Standesbeamten mit Unterschrift und Siegel
18 Juli 1912 N° Breslau II 1644/12		Wichorzyk

Anmerkung: Die kirchlichen Einsichtigungen in Beziehung auf Taufe und Trauung werden hierdurch nicht berührt.

II. Kinder

A Geburten

Laufende Nr.	Vor- und Zunamen	Zeit u. Ort der Geburt	Standesamt und Nr. des Geburtsregisters	Beglaubigung des Standesbeamten mit Unterschrift und Siegel
5.	Laika Margot Ruth Wolframs	18. November 1912 Breslau	Breslau V 2049	i.A. [signature]
6.				
7.				
8.				

B Todesfälle

Zeit und Ort des Todes	Standesamt und Nr. des Sterberegisters	Beglaubigung des Standesbeamten mit Unterschrift und Siegel

Anmerkung: Die kirchlichen Zertifikationen in Beziehung auf Taufe und Trauung werden hierdurch nicht berührt.

The author's father, Jakob Wolfsohn in 1939, one month after his release from Buchenwald.

The author's mother, Irene Wolfson (Wolfsohn), celebrated on this bus card from 1952 in Portland, Oregon.

Breslau City Hall

A drawing by the author's mother, Irene Wolfsohn.

The author's maternal grandfather in Zobten in 1936.

The author, Frank, as indicated by the arrow and caption on the photograph, in the sixth grade in Breslau (1929-1930).

Another photo of Frank, at the Landheim School, in the second row as indicated by the arrow. You just barely see the top half of his face, obscured by the front row.

A postcard of Zobten from a family member
postmarked June 7, 1937.

A photograph taken by the author on a return trip to the
former Wolfsohn country home in Zobten in 1974.

Breslau Administrative District in Silesia

The Breslau administrative district in the province of Silesia in the early Twentieth century. The map also indicates the proximity of Breslau to Zobten, approximately nineteen miles apart.

The author, Frank, 20 years old, far right, playing cards with his family on the veranda of the Wolfsohn country home in Zobten, 19 miles southwest of Breslau, 1938.

The author's older sister, Steffi, in Elbeuf, France during the war.

The author, Frank (as indicated by the arrow, seated at the left in the front row), having completed basic training at Camp Wolters just outside of Mineral Wells, Texas in 1944. During World War II, Camp Wolters was the largest infantry replacement training center in the United States. Shortly after this photograph was taken, Frank would be assigned to service in Germany as a driver and interpreter.

The New Recruit

Frank Wesley just before going overseas in 1944.

Pvt. Frank Wesley, second from left, with the U.S. Army Liaison Staff (#5). The Liaison Staff was a unit whose purpose was to assist other friendly forces and Allied armies.

Frank with the Liaison Staff command car.

The author, Frank, at Brenner Pass, the mountain crossing from Italy into Nazi Germany.

American soldiers on a terrace in Vegesack at the captured headquarters of the Nazi Luftwaffe. Vegesack was located on the Weser River just outside of Bremen.

Bremen

The centerpoint of Bremen a few days after Bremen's surrender.

Bremen in rubble after the May 1945 bombing. Bremen was one of the last Allied battles of the European war.

Frank in Bremen, May 1945.

Surrender

Along the seawall on the beach south of Cuxhaven. Frank escorting a surrendering Nazi officer to receive his surrender terms.

Ljubljana

The author attending the XV International Congress of Applied Psychology, August 2–8, 1964, at the University of Ljubljana in former Yugoslavia. This postwar conference was celebrated for marking the first occasion in which both Eastern and Western countries participated together.

October 1965 Portland, Oregon

Front row, l. to r., Werner, Steffi, Frank, and Ruth. Irene is behind her children. The year this photograph was taken represents the first time all four siblings were reunited since the start of WWII in Europe, almost 30 years.

The photograph was taken in Irene Wolfson's backyard looking toward downtown Portland.

Haupt Bahnhof

The author boarding a train at the main train station in Wrocław (formerly Breslau) for Sobótka (formerly Zobten) in 1974 on his first return visit since childhood. What was once part of Germany, Breslau was annexed to Poland after World War II, a result of the Yalta and Potsdam conferences of 1945.

Frank at 95

Frank addressing and entertaining friends and family at his 95th birthday party in 2013. Always the home boy, Frank is sporting a new souvenir T-shirt from Wrocław (formerly Breslau).

The Original Introduction

The following document is the third revision to the original introduction for this book. In comparison, the final introduction included in the front of this book has a more concise and focused tone in what one should expect in the chapters that follow it.

It is interesting to note however, hence the reason for its historical inclusion here, that the following original introduction, with its somewhat broader coverage, also served as a paper (along with oral elaboration) presented by the author in numerous lectures and presentations during the time in which the book was being written.

Third Revision

Did Hitler Win?

Hitler committed suicide in April 1945 and a month later the last remnants of his army surrendered. German cities laid in ruins and displaced persons roamed the countryside. Since that time half a century has passed and I have often asked myself if, in certain respects, Hitler did not win the war. From his earliest campaign speeches in Munich until his final testament in his Berlin bunker, Hitler espoused three major aims. To rid Germany of the Jews, to destroy Bolshevism, and to make Germany a world power.

Germany is now a major economic power and bolshevism has disintegrated. Though both of these events came true they did not happen in Hitler's spirit. Hitler planned to destroy bolshevism by making all Slavs vassals of Germany and to use Germany's world power to enslave non-Aryan nations. Contrary to Hitler's wishes both of these events, Germany's rise and bolshevism's fall from power, have contributed to freedom and democracy. It is, however, very questionable whether Hitler's major wish to rid Germany of its Jews, which has almost become a reality, had any such beneficial effects.

After Hitler was defeated, few surviving Jews returned to Germany settling mostly in other Western countries and in the newly founded state of Israel. From all of Hitler's victims, the Jews in Israel have had the least peaceful lives. Half a century after Hitler's demise, their country is still dependent on foreign arms and peace with their neighbors is still not in sight.

There were several reasons why the German Jews did not return. About half of them had lived in parts of Germany which the Allies deeded to Poland or East Germany. Had they returned, they would have had to live under communism. Furthermore, as soon as West Germany's financial system was reestablished, Hitler's victims were paid reparations for loss of property and health. These payments were also made to victims living in foreign countries and were often sufficient to pay for one's livelihood there, without the necessity of moving back to Germany.

The major reason for the Jews' reluctance to return, however, was a psychological one. A few months before the war ended, the Russian army liberated several death camps in Eastern Poland and their photos substantiated the worst fears of the Jews and the world at large. Pictures and eyewitness reports of soldiers and survivors showed that millions of European Jews were systematically exterminated in Auschwitz and in a dozen other death camps. Captured Gestapo documents showed that the rounding up of the European Jews, their transports to the ghettos, and later to the death camps in Poland, were planned in detail and carried out with clockwork precision. Because the search for the Jews was so thorough and the transports and the killings went on for three full years (1941-1944), it is easy to believe that every German must have had a hand in it. Thus, Jews throughout the world became convinced that Germans had always hated the Jews and will always hate them in the future. To a large extent this belief has lasted until the present. It has perhaps been reinforced by the Zionists' idea that all Jews who live in diaspora, outside Israel, are second-class citizens, and those who live in Germany are worse than second-class. As the Jerusalem historian, Mosche Zimmermann reports, they are considered living in "diaspora in the land of murderers." (Spiegel, Jan. 20, 1992).

Reflecting on the history of the German Jews, I shall attempt to show that there was less anti-Semitism in pre-Hitler Germany than in most other European countries, and that the majority of Germans did not vote for Hitler. I shall also show that once Hitler came to power, neither the German gentiles nor the world at large helped the Jews. Not because they hated the Jews, but because they did not realize the looming danger. Neither did we German Jews foresee our impending doom. Our close relationship with German non-Jews and the democratic principle instilled in us, having lived in Germany for generations, convinced us that we would never lose our rights as human beings. Along with 1,000 other Jews, even as

I was marched through the streets of Breslau (now Wroclaw) by shouting Storm Troopers during the first mass-arrests in 1938, I still believed that the Gestapo who had arrested us had gone mad and that we would be justly treated at our destination, wherever that would be. All hopes were immediately shattered when our train halted in the middle of the night and we were ordered to jump out, beaten with whips and clubs while running single file through the gates of Buchenwald Concentration Camp.

The physical pain was great. There was little food and hardly any water for the first few days, and no shelter during cold mid-November nights. My psychological pain was just as unbearable. Why had I and thousands of other Jews lived under Hitler's regime for almost six years, (from 1933 to 1938), and did not immigrate. Why didn't I and most others know that Buchenwald and several other concentration camps existed. At daybreak our remorse and fears reached new heights. We saw rows of permanent barracks and thousands of emaciated and haggard prisoners standing in motionless rows to be counted before being marched out to their work sites. Almost all of these inmates were German gentiles, and many of them had already been in the camp for one or two years.

I came from a well educated family, went to German schools, and had close friends among Germans of different social strata and religions. I, and most Germans, had known that the concentration camp Dachau existed since 1934 and we believed that it was a camp for those who actively resisted the Nazi movement. We did not know that by 1938, ten other camps had been established holding about 100,000 inmates. I believe that most German gentiles had likewise thought the vast majority of the inmates at that time were German gentiles and not Jews, and had no knowledge of the extent of the camps and their internal torturous conditions.

After the war ended it was generally believed that most Germans knew about the camps and their conditions, and stood idly by. Ironically, most Germans first became aware of the camps during the mass arrests in November, 1938, when they saw the synagogues burning, store windows smashed, and thousands of Jews being marched through town to "unknown destinations." Orchestrated by the propaganda minister, Goebbels, it all happened suddenly during the night of November 9th in 1938—a night which became known as the Crystal Night, because the main streets of most major German cities were littered with broken window glass. While the Gentiles had been sent to concentration camps one by one, the Jews were sent there with great fanfare, accompanied by siren noises, guarded by mounted police and torch-carrying storm Troopers.

The actual conditions which existed in the camps were never revealed to the public. Few of us who were released from a camp dared to talk about its inhuman conditions and the high death rates. Before anyone was released, he was warned that a single word about the camp would mean a return to the camp. News about the camp which did leak out was immediately countered by the Nazi propaganda machine as lies spread by the International Jewish hatemonger press. Even after I arrived in the U.S. in 1939, I was extremely careful whom I told about my camp experiences. I still had relatives in Germany and feared that they might be subjected to reprisals. At that time, neither inside nor outside Germany, did people know or believe that thousands of German gentiles and Jews were starved, beaten, and slowly worked to death inside a dozen German concentration camps.

As late as June, 1939, (three months before the war started), for instance, President Roosevelt refused to grant asylum to 915 Jews who were on the German liner, St. Louis. Though all Jews had obtained legitimate entry visas for Cuba, they were forbidden to debark after the liner entered Havana harbor. Also, several attempts by refugee committees to obtain permission for them to enter the U.S. failed in spite of the fact that it was known that the ship's captain had orders to return all passengers to a special concentration camp in Hamburg in case he could not find asylum for them.

Once World War II started in September, 1939, transports to prisons, labor and concentration camps became more visible. But at the same time, any verbal displeasure or physical interference with the war effort were categorized as treason. "Volksjustice" courts, operated by local party officials could hand out prison or death sentences. Being friendly to a Jew (Judenfreundlich) was often a sufficient charge. In some instances scores of citizens were killed to avenge the death of a single Nazi.

Even after the war started, the Nazis were still trying to deflect their guilt from persecuting the Jews by forcing a "self-administration" on them. The Chief Rabbi, Leo Baeck, head of the Association of German Jews, was made responsible for all Jewish matters. His office was given the task to distribute food rations and to execute all orders given to him by the Gestapo. He had no power to ask for more rations, nor to alter any orders given to him. It was eventually the "Jewish Internal Police" who had to march the Jews to the rail heads for their final transports to Poland. The Gestapo designed this ruse to give the Germans and even some of the victimized Jews the impression that the Jews inflicted their misery upon themselves. In the following chapters it will be described how Heinrich Himmler, Hitler's main architect for the extermination of the Jews, kept all aspects of it a strict secret. He did not trust the anti-Semitism of the Germans. He warned them repeatedly never to trust any Jew, emphasizing that Jews appeared individually as very nice people, but planned to destroy the German race collectively. To play it safe, Himmler established all death camps in Poland, away from the sight of Germans and away from the reach of Allied planes. In Poland, Himmler would clear entire villages of their inhabitants, Gentiles and Jews, by sending them to forced labor in Germany, thereby gaining large areas for factory, labor, and death camp complexes.

Furthermore, the Gestapo coded all orders referring to labor and death camps. The initials S.B., for instance, stood for "Spezial Behandlung", or special treatment, which meant: "to be shot or gassed upon arrival." One high ranking Nazi medical officer got the order from Himmler to treat 70,000 Poles like Jews because they had tuberculosis. The officer wrote a long letter to Hitler pleading for the lives of these patients, mentioning that it was wrong to kill these Poles, and he actually used the word "kill". When Himmler found out that he did not use the code S.B., he ordered the officer himself be sent to a concentration camp for the duration of the war.

Using secret codes and isolated locations, the Nazis were able to keep the evidence of their wholesale exterminations away from the world for several years. Not until 1942, did Polish train personnel inform the British Broadcasting Corporation through their underground army, that Jews were killed in certain camps. The underground knew that 130,000 Jews had been sent to Belzec, and they also knew that this camp could not possibly hold that many people, even if they stood shoulder to shoulder. The BBC, however, did not broadcast this report.

Not only did the Nazis try to keep the camp conditions a secret, they additionally spread false information. One concentration camp, Theresienstadt (Terezin) was designated as a "showplace" for the International Red Cross. But even there inmates had to work 100 hours per week and live with six others in one small room. Periodically, they were forced to write dictated messages to their acquaintances on the outside, that they were healthy and well, though they were starving and dying of malnutrition.

Another ruse was used by the S.S. killing commandos who followed the advances of the German army into the newly conquered Russian cities in order to shoot the Jewish population. The S.S. used posters depicting ideal labor camp conditions in Germany and asked all Jews to assemble outside the city limits to await transport to Germany. The transports never came. Towards the evening, the Jews were marched to nearby tank defense ditches and machine-gunned. About a million Eastern Jews found their death in that treacherous and cruel way.

As already mentioned, the Jews in general consider the Germans guilty for knowing about the camps and for allowing their existence. But, as I have indicated and will discuss in more detail in the following chapters, most Germans, including most Jews, as well as the world at large, had little knowledge about the number nor about the internal conditions of the camps. Knowledge did leak out over a 10-year period, beginning with Dachau established in 1934, until the liberation of Auschwitz early in 1945. During this decade, the Nazis were always one step ahead of those who wanted to or did resist them. They were ahead in their propaganda, in their diplomacy, and in their military might, until their first severe setback at Stalingrad early in 1943 when the Russians captured 24 German generals and 180,000 men. (German reports listed only 90,000).

Aside from guilt by omission, knowing but not acting, many Jews considered the Germans guilty because they voted for Hitler and let him come to power. I shall also discuss why many Germans voted for Hitler, though they did not wish the Jews any harm. In his early campaign speeches Hitler linked bolshevism to Judaism, leaving many Germans, Gentiles and Jews, with the impression that he hated the bolshevists more than the Jews. Publicly, he announced at times that the Jews and Germans can live in peace if they separate. But as some of the Nurnberg documents showed, in private among his aids, he wished to see all Jews starving in an enclosure where they would tear themselves apart in their struggle for food.

Hitler's public and private behavior can be compared to that of David Duke who ran for Governor of Louisiana in 1991. In public, Duke reiterated that his anti-Semitism was a thing of the past and that he believed Jews and Gentile can live peacefully side by side. In private, however, he had mentioned to a reporter, that the Jews and Negroes are only good for their ashes. Half of the white population of Louisiana did vote for Duke, mostly in good faith for better economic conditions, and not because they wished to see the Jews tortured and burnt.

Hitler not only tricked the German voters, but also some Italian and British diplomats who allowed him to build up his war machinery as a bulwark against bolshevism. In addition, Hitler was indirectly aided by France and the United States by not granting Germany an earlier moratorium on the war debts. This caused high unemployment rates and food shortages and an increase in votes for Hitler's party. While Hitler convinced the Western powers that he stood firmly against bolshevism, he signed a secret friendship-pact with Stalin, agreeing to a surprise attack on Poland with Germany taking over the western half and Russia, the eastern half.

Hitler was never inconspicuous. Even when his party was small, its members wore uniforms and caused frequent disturbances by trying to break up demonstrations held by the communists and socialists. Hitler gave frequent hour-long speeches. He usually shouted at the top of his lungs, repeating insult after insult at bolshevists, capitalists, Jews and the Allies who had forced Germany to give up some of its territory and pay reparations after World War I.

Few people took Hitler seriously during his rise to power. At different times he was imprisoned, forbidden to assemble and to wear the Nazi uniform. Each time, however, he resurfaced somewhat stronger by hiding behind or by circumventing the freedoms the German constitution guaranteed. When his Brown Shirts were forbidden to assemble, he created the Black Shirts, the Storm Troopers, who later became his elite body guards.

People became accustomed to Hitler's rantings, considering him a crank and rabble-rouser. Few believed that he could ever rise to power. There were other factors which reinforced this belief. Germany's economic and military affairs were largely dictated by the Allies in the Treaty of Versailles at the end of World War I, in 1918. Since Hitler vowed to annul this treaty, one had reason to believe that the Allies would never allow Hitler's party to become a military power. My mother, who had studied economics at the University of Breslau and who had many close friends active in the Central Catholic and Socialist parties, would often say, "The Allies will never permit it." That was the opinion of most Germans.

As had happened throughout the history of party systems, in economic depressions, voters would favor those leaders who promise food and work. How these goals are reached becomes a secondary matter, be it through oppression of a class, a race, or by conquering other nations. Hitler's plan to gain back some of the territory Germany had lost and to stop paying Germany's war debts were, at the time, plausible solutions for Germany's economic plight. Many of us German Jews could have supported these two points of the Nazi party program.

Hitler's party grew during the depression of the late 20's, when close to 10% of Germany's working force became unemployed. The workers looked more closely at both the Nazi and the Communist parties. Both promised work and both gained votes. Consequently, some industrialists, fearing Stalin more than Hitler, gave large sums of money to Hitler's party. Hitler used part of this money to reinforce his elite body guards which he employed to intimidate and to assassinate opposition forces in his own party, anti-Nazi generals, and diplomats in foreign countries. Germany had a multi-party system with six major and, at any given time, approximately ten minor parties. Hitler's party never received a majority of votes. Only after a coalition with a smaller rightist party was Hitler appointed Chancellor. Within weeks after his appointment, he declared marshal law and by arresting some of the opposition leaders on treason charges, his party gained parliamentary majority. In terms of votes, only about a third of the German people voted for Hitler and perhaps only half of those did so to satisfy any anti-Semitic desires. After the first mass arrest of Jews during the Crystal Night in 1938, both the American and the British embassies reported to their respective governments that the German people showed much restraint by not participating in the boycott and riots.

Showing that the German public was not anti-Semantic, and that they did not actively participate in isolating the Jews or in sending them to their death camps, shall in no way diminish the magnitude nor the guilt of the hideous crimes committed by Hitler's machinery. Hitler began his political career by joining a small group of fanatical anti-Semites. He founded the Brown Shirts, and later the Black Shirts. By 1930, the Black Shirts numbered 15,000. Several hundred of them swore a special oath and became Hitler's "Elite" body guards. During the war, the Black Shirts, called the S.S., had grown to over one million. They furnished the manpower for the Gestapo, the Secret Police, the concentration camp guards, the Killing Commandos, and a special unit of attack front soldiers, the "Weapon SS."

The fact that a relatively small minority could ultimately terrorize almost all of Europe and put millions of innocent people to death, should not comfort us in any way. To the contrary, it should warn us against present and future dictators. In Saddam Hussein, the world has now seen a dictator, similar to Hitler, who expanded a relatively small group into the Republican Guards, which in turn caused a disproportionately large amount of death and environmental damage.

Index

A

Anti-Semitism
  Anti-Semitic League 9
  conditioned anti-Semitism 33
  in France 7–8
  in Germany 3–4
  in Rumania 48–50
  in Russia 7
  in the Middle Ages 1–5
  Pre-Nazi 7–9
  Semitic anti-Semitism 8
  staged anti-Semitism 27–31
Antonescu, Ion 48–50
Arrests 31, 34, 43, 54, 60, 64, 65, 68, 70
Auschwitz. *See* Concentration camps

B

Baeck, Dr. Leo 74
Bain, A. 8, 99
Barkai, Avraham 28, 99
Baynes, Norman H. 22, 29, 36, 37, 52, 99
Berlin 7, 9, 14, 23, 24, 29, 49, 60, 61, 63, 69, 71, 75, 77, 85
Bieber, H. 11, 99
Black, Edwin 15, 28, 99
Black Shirts 64, 69

Bolshevists 19, 34, 77, 91
Boycott 27, 28, 51, 74
Breslau 7, 14, 23, 31, 55, 61, 68, 75, 82
Broszat, Martin 34, 36, 43, 65, 78, 79, 99
Brown Shirts 17, 24, 27, 28, 64, 65
  dissolution 67–69
Brutalities 39, 42, 43, 47. *See the entirety of* Chapter Eight, Conditioned Brutality; *See the entirety of* Chapter Ten, Non-German Brutalities

C

Central Verein 59, 73, 100
Chamberlain, Houston Stewart 15
Chamberlain, Neville 70–72, 93
Cohen, Hermann 8
Communism 15, 23, 66, 72
  arrests of 33–36, 63–66
  fear of 25
  take over attempts 22, 33
Communist Party 22
Concentration camps
  Auschwitz 48, 49, 60, 77–80, 91
  Buchenwald 9, 20, 41, 42, 44, 45, 55, 60, 73, 82

Dachau 40, 65, 66
Eicke prototype 40
Koch, commandant 42
Lodz 77, 78
Theresienstadt 60, 77
Concordat 70
Cranston, U.S. Sen. Alan 74
Crystal Night 30, 31, 35, 47, 52–54, 60, 73, 74, 81, 93
Czechoslovakia 35, 70, 71, 72, 77, 81, 84, 85, 88

D

Daladier, Eduard 70, 93
Dawidowicz, Lucy 38, 100
Deportations 49, 75, 77
Destruction 7, 35, 64, 66, 70, 78, 81–83, 86
Deutsche, W. 8, 100
Dostoevsky 7
Dreyfus Affair 7

E

Eichmann, Adolf 48
Eicke, Theodore 39–41
Emigration 30, 51, 55, 94
  forbidden 75
  Goering's order 93
  Hilfsverein 7
  Madagascar plan 53, 94
  Nations of Asylum 51–55
  Rublee plan 93
England 2, 3, 4, 28, 29, 35, 54, 67, 70, 71, 72, 81, 84, 99
Ettinger, S. 7, 100

F

Fest, Joachim 17, 21, 25, 70, 95, 100
First World War 60, 91. See also World War I

Ford, Henry 15, 16
France 1, 2, 3, 4, 7, 21, 25, 35, 52, 53, 54, 71, 72, 81, 82, 86, 88
Frank, Hans 79
Freeden, Herbert 30, 100
Friedjung, Heinrich 8
Friedlaender, Saul 92
"Friendship Pact" 70

G

Gay, Ruth 100
German-Jewish symbiosis 11–14
German public schools 13
Gilman, Sander 9, 100
Gobineau, Joseph de 15, 100
Goebbels, Joseph 27, 29, 30, 31, 33, 36, 52, 74, 85, 93, 95
Goering, Hermann 17, 28, 30, 33, 35, 63–65, 67, 92, 93
Goldhagen, Daniel 1, 2, 5, 7, 11, 12, 16, 21, 22, 28, 31, 33, 37, 39, 42, 43, 45, 47, 50, 66, 72, 81, 85, 91, 94, 95, 100

H

Hackett, David A. 41, 44, 100
Hebrew 102
  translations 11
Heins, H. 17, 100
Herzl, Theodor 7, 8
Heydrich, Reinhard 33, 43, 68, 74–78, 83–85, 92, 94
Hilberg, Raul 24, 49, 77, 83, 100, 102
Hilderbrand, Klaus 63, 100
Hilfsverein. See Jewish Aid Society
Himmler, Heinrich 17, 37, 38, 40, 42, 65, 67–69, 79, 84, 93
  ghetto destruction 88
  Minsk address 78
  Posen address 37, 78

Hindenburg, Paul von 33, 63
Hitler, Adolf 1, 9, 19, 60, 63, 73, 81, 83, 91, 95, 96, 101
  Anti-Christianity 16–17
  Antisemitism 15–20, 33–37
  early speeches 15, 21
  invasions 70–72, 82, 94
  Mein Kampf 15–18, 21, 74
  Nations of Asylum conference 52–53
  opposition arrests 64–66
  propaganda 93
  psychosexuality 18
  Roehm execution 67–69
  staged anti-Semitism 27–31
  voting for 21–25
Hitler Youth 23, 24, 39, 40
Hoffmann, P. 72, 101
Holocaust 1, 5, 19, 47
  early development 21
Höss, R. 101
Hugh of Lincoln 2

I

Isopescu, Modest 49

J

Jehovah's Witnesses 44, 45, 67
Jewish Aid Society 7
Jewish Order Service 75, 85, 86
Jewish Problem 2, 8. *See also* Jewish Question
Jewish Question 8, 9
Jewish Self-Administration 74, 85, 92
Jews
  assimilation 8
  councils 92
  Eastern Jews 8, 34, 60, 83, 100
  Frontline Veterans 60
  in Middle Ages 1–5
  Judenkartei 92

Kulturbund 30, 92
Patriotism 59, 60
Reformed Judaism 8, 13, 14
Self-Administration 74, 75, 85, 92
Judenpolizei 86

K

Kaznelson, Siegmund 13, 101
Koch, Sgt. Karl 41, 42
Kracauer, I. 4, 101
Krausnick, Helmut 30, 47, 101, 103
Kristallnacht. *See* Crystal Night
Krueger, Kurt 18, 101
Kulturbund 30, 92

L

Labor camps 41, 75, 77, 79, 84, 85, 87, 88
Langmuir, Gavin I. 2, 101
Laqueur, Walter 101
League of Nations 21
Lessing, Ephraim 11
Lidice 84
Lipstadt, Deborah E. 74, 101
Lodz 77, 78
Long, Wellington 17, 101
Luther, Martin 4, 101

M

MacDonald, Callum A. 83, 101
Madagascar 53, 94
Marrus, Michael R. 7, 21
McKale, Donald 48, 102
Mein Kampf. *See* Hitler, Adolf
Mendelsohn, Moses 11–13
Munich 18, 24, 61, 68, 70, 72, 91, 92, 93

N

National League of Jewish Frontline Veterans 60
National Liberation Party 12
Nations of Asylum 51, 52
Nazi Party 24, 33, 39, 47
  founding 22
  propaganda 23, 24
  votes 21, 59, 61
Netherlands
  Dutch Nazi Party 47
  Dutch SS 83
  fines 83
  Holland 47, 52, 54, 88
    bombings 82
    transports from 77
Niewyk, Donald 11, 60, 102
Night and Fog 86
Nurnberg Laws 9–10, 18–20, 29–32

O

Ostjuden (Eastern Jews) 8

P

Papen, Franz von 19, 20, 22, 63, 69
Paulus, Gen. Friedrich 95
"Peace In Our Time" 70
Pogroms 2, 7
Poland 42, 55, 70, 72, 73, 75, 79, 81, 83, 85, 91, 92, 94, 95
Poles 16, 17, 44, 45, 60, 61, 78, 79, 85, 86
Pre-Hitler Youth 23
Pulzer, Peter 2, 102

Q

Quisling, Yidkum 47

R

Ragins, Sanford 102
Rassenschande 18
Reform Judaism. *See* Jews, Reformed Judaism
Reichsbanner 24
Reichstags fire 33, 70
Reitlinger, Gerald 48, 78, 87, 102
Remak, Joachim 16, 102
Ribbentrop, J. von 53, 102
Rinott, M. 7, 102
Ritual Trial 2
Roehm, Ernst 17, 40, 67, 68, 69, 72, 91
Rublee plan 93
Russia 8, 22, 25, 36, 48, 50, 70, 72, 82, 83, 85, 94, 100, 102
  anti-Semitism 7
  friendship pact 91
  pogroms 7
  prisoners 42, 94

S

Schapiro, Leonard 7, 102
Schechtman, Joseph 102
Scheffler, Wolfgang 22, 59, 102
Scholom, Gershom 8, 102
Schwarzschild, Steven 103
Slavs 16
Sterling, E. 2, 103
Symbiosis. *See* German-Jewish symbiosis

T

Theodore Eicke 39
Treitschke, Heinrich 9

U

Ukrainian Jews 11

V

Versailles Treaty 25
Vice Chancellory 63

W

Wagner, Richard 15
Warsaw ghetto 87
Weimar Republic 11, 13, 21, 22, 24,
    33, 39, 60, 61
Wiedemann, F. 35, 103
World War I 15, 21, 22, 25. *See
    also* First World War

X

Xanten trial 3

Y

Yiddish translations 11

Z

Zionism 102
  Zionist Party 87